There is a massive, urgent problem facing the Church today. Though largely overlooked, the consequences are eternal for countless millions. With all the authority of heaven and earth, the Lord Jesus Christ gave his people one single task to accomplish in the Church Age: Bring the gospel to all nations. And yet, two thousand years later, there are still at least two billion people who have never heard of the only way of salvation. More troubling, the number of unreached has been increasing over the past century and will continue to rise unless there is a change in the trend. Fortunately, God has provided the solution and has given us the joy and privilege of being part of that solution. So the World Will Know *explores how and why the number of unreached continues to rise. More to the point, it explores the Lord's solution to the problem. It is a wake-up call for every Christian.*

Praise for So the World Will Know

"A must-read not only for every pastor but also for every Christian."

> As one who has dedicated my whole life to Christ's mission, who has been an eyewitness to God's Spirit at work among Iranians, who has served on multiple mission boards, and who has preached at dozens of mission conferences, I wish I had had a copy of J. Christopher Evans's *So the World Will Know*. As I read his book, I found my heart strangely touched, for I was confronted with what I had always believed but was never able to articulate as well as he has. His careful research and heartwarming illustrations kept me glued to every page. My first impulse was to want to send a copy of his book to every pastor I knew. His inspired book, in my opinion, is a must-read not only for every pastor but also for every Christian.
>
> <div align="right">—Rev. Tat Stewart, director emeritus of Persian ministries for the Associate Reformed Presbyterian Church; author of <i>No Stranger: To Iran, Its People and Its Church</i>; co-founder, SAT-7 PARS</div>

"Evans's testimony, and that of others mentioned in the book, will warm hearts and inform minds."

> Evans is interested and involved in new forms of reaching those unreached, whether in terms of distance, culture, or language.

Traditional TV ministry is one such involvement, but so are the various forms of social media. J. Christopher Evans's testimony, and that of others mentioned in the book, will warm hearts and inform minds. I pray it will encourage many to pray, to give, and to go.

—Msgr. Dr. Michael Nazir-Ali, president,
Oxford Centre for Training, Research, Advocacy & Dialogue

"A must-read for believers and Church leaders alike who are looking to make a meaningful impact in their communities and beyond."

In *So the World Will Know*, J. Christopher Evans offers an insightful and compelling guide for anyone passionate about sharing the gospel. This book goes behind the mechanics of evangelism and dives deep into the essence of what it means to communicate the vision of Christ for his Church. Through personal anecdotes, surveys, broader societal themes, and real-life stories, Evans equips readers with both the heart and the tools to reach others effectively and authentically.

Whether you are new to evangelism or a seasoned believer, this book challenges you to embrace a lifestyle of outreach, grounded in compassion and truth. It is a must-read for believers and Church leaders alike who are looking to make a meaningful impact on their communities and beyond.

—Dr. David Wong, founding pastor,
Washington International Church and People Without Borders

So the World Will Know

Jesus' Game-Changing Vision for World Evangelization & Your Part in It

J. Christopher Evans

So the World Will Know: Jesus' Game-Changing Vision for World Evangelization & Your Part in It
Copyright © 2025 J. Christopher Evans

Published by I-AM Press

All rights reserved. No part of this publication may be reproduced, stored in a retrieval system or transmitted in any form by any means, electronic, mechanical, photocopy, recording or otherwise, without the prior permission of the publisher, except as provided by USA copyright law.

Cover art: *Jesus Christ, the Great High Priest*, by Mark Lawrence, copyright 2021, used by permission.

Printed in the United States of America

Unless otherwise indicated, all Scripture references are from The Holy Bible, English Standard Version, copyright © 2001 by Crossway Bibles, a division of Good News Publishers. All rights reserved. All emphases within Scripture quotations have been added by the author.

NO AI TRAINING: Without in any way limiting the author's and publisher's exclusive rights under copyright, any use of this publication to "train" generative artificial intelligence (AI) technologies to generate text is expressly prohibited. The author reserves all rights to license uses of this work for generative AI training and development of machine learning language models.

Some names and places have been changed for security purposes.

ISBN 979-8-9990720-0-9 (hardcover)
ISBN 979-8-9990720-1-6 (paperback)
ISBN 979-8-9990720-2-3 (ebook)
ISBN 979-8-9990720-3-0 (PDF)

DEDICATED TO GOD THE Father Almighty, who chose us in love before he created the universe and who sent his only Son into the world to redeem us even by his blood.

To Jesus Christ our Lord, who came into the world to become the Lamb of God and take away our sins. In doing so, he revealed the glory of God, vindicated his honor, and forever conquered evil.

To God the Holy Spirit, who has made these things known to us, given us eternal life, and empowered us to make this glorious gospel known among all nations with joy.

To him I dedicate this book for his greater glory and the advance of the gospel among the nations.

The first Reformation gave the Word of God to the people of God; we need a Second Reformation to give the work of God to the people of God.
—Ford Maddox

Contents

How the Lord Unexpectedly Led Us to Start a Media Ministry for the Unreached   1

The Jonah Paradigm   9

PART ONE
THE PROBLEM:
THE NUMBER OF UNREACHED IS INCREASING

1. The Number of Unreached is Increasing   17

2. Why the Number of Unreached is Increasing   25
    CASE STUDY: MOHAMAD, IRANIAN MINISTER OF THE GOSPEL

3. How the Church Came to Marginalize Her Mission Even Though the Mission of God is the Bible's Central Theme   47

PART TWO
THE SOLUTION:
CHRIST'S VISION FOR HIS MISSION

4. What the Bible is Really All About   63

5. Is the Great Commission Only for Professional Missionaries?   71
    CASE STUDY: JEREMIAH, AFRICAN FARMER AND TENTMAKER

6. Jesus' Vision for the Mission: The Last Discourse—A Blueprint for the Last Command   87

PART THREE
IMPLICATIONS

7. Working Together as the Body of Christ   105

8. The Power of Our United Witness   115

9. Every Christian a Missionary?   119

   CASE STUDY: DAVE, AMERICAN RETIREE AND TENTMAKER

10. The Higher Purpose of Your Vocation   131

    CASE STUDY: STEVE, AMERICAN DOCTOR AND TENTMAKER

PART FOUR
APPLICATIONS

11. The Problem of Evil, God's Sovereignty, and the Advance of the Gospel   147

12. Praying Together for Revival and Reformation   157

    CASE STUDY: SARAH AND SOLOMON, MIDDLE EASTERN TENTMAKER PASTORS

13. Working Together as the Body of Christ   177

14. Your Identity as a Witness   181

15. For Every Follower of Christ: Your Vocation as a Ministry   185

    CASE STUDY: MARIANA, SOUTH AMERICAN PHYSICAL THERAPIST AND TENTMAKER

16. For Christian Leaders: Your Crucial Role   197

17. The Real "Mission From God" Appeal   205

    CASE STUDY: JOHN, AMERICAN CEO AND TENTMAKER

Appendices   213

Notes   233

Bibliography   239

About the Author   247

Preface

How the Lord Unexpectedly Led Us to Start a Media Ministry for the Unreached

STARTING A MEDIA MINISTRY for an unreached country wasn't just outside my wheelhouse. It was laughably impossible for me. But God had other plans.

I was a very unlikely founder of a media ministry. I knew little about the country I'll call "Khorastan" for security reasons. I knew even less about media ministry, using television and social media to evangelize those who have never heard the Good News. I was not very good at being part of an organization, much less leading one. I have never considered myself to be a leader. Not only that, I was already ten years into retirement. But I sensed the irresistible call of Christ to see the gospel advance among Khorastan's unreached millions. Isn't that just like the Lord? He can choose the most unlikely people to do his bidding. Sometimes he deliberately chooses the foolish things of this world so there is no room for boasting. And I was "Exhibit A"!

It was 2013, and I had the privilege of serving as head of the strategy committee of a denominational mission board in the US. It had sent over one hundred missionaries to Khorastan in the previous one hundred years. But now, the number of missionaries had dwindled down to two families, and the government wasn't issuing new visas for missionaries.

It was tempting just to take the path of least resistance: pack up and go home. But Khorastan had millions in unreached groups who had no access to the only way of salvation. It is a Muslim-majority country. The few who are Christians are among the most oppressed and persecuted believers in the world.

The task before our committee was to come up with a strategy for continuing to carry out Christ's Great Commission in this nation in an era when we could no longer send conventional missionaries. We had a number of legacy missions—ministries that had developed over the past century. We had a hospital and schools, but nothing explicitly designed to make the gospel known in Khorastan, which has such a massive, desperate need. The problem was we wanted to do more than just provide excellent healthcare and education for a few. We wanted to make eternal life available to many.

While these fine ministries did excellent work, they were not specifically designed to carry out the Great Commission, let alone meet the demands of making Christ known in such a large country with such a large number of unreached people. What to do?

One day at a board meeting, one of our missionaries shared a video about what God was doing in Iran. I was amazed at how he was using a Christian satellite-television ministry for Iran, easily bypassing government censorship in order to support a powerful move of God in that country. Iran was showing the greatest rate of church growth in the world, about 17–19%, in spite of severe repression and persecution from the government. Why couldn't God do the same in the Khorastan?

Instead of the government hindering church growth, God was actually using the very unpopular government in Iran to accelerate the growth of the church. When the government announced a crackdown on this media ministry, the response from the average Iranian on the street was, "If the government is against it, I'd better go check it out!" The government crackdowns backfired so spectacularly that it has been said that the Supreme Leader is worth ten Billy Grahams in terms of bringing people to Christ!

The government could ban missionaries, forbid church attendance, and outlaw conversion to Christ. But they were powerless to stop the move of Almighty God, the exploding house church movement, and the Christian satellite broadcasts that could easily bypass government censorship and control.

In relation to Khorastan, my thought was that we should shift from working directly to working indirectly—that we should mobilize the nationals to evangelize their own countrymen. I also thought we should transition from old-school methods, such as Bible correspondence schools, to harnessing the power of modern communications tools, such as television, the Internet, and social media.

My pastor read the strategy paper I wrote about mobilizing the Church in Khorastan, and responded by saying, "What we need is a game changer—something like a satellite television channel."

After this, I began to meet with one of the founders of the Iranian media ministry to find out how this kind of ministry works and how they started it. He helped me understand how developing the vision and sharing it would draw people in. That, in turn, would bring in the necessary resources. This fit in with something I already understood about leadership. **The essence of leadership is articulating a vision and seeing it realized. So, I began to realize that Christian leadership was about bringing people into Jesus' vision and seeing it realized.**

He also suggested I attend their annual partner's fundraising and networking meeting in the Middle East in 2014. He connected me with the founder of the coalition-based media ministry for the Middle East and North Africa. These meetings were eye-opening.

At one partner's meeting, a woman from Iran testified how her drug-addicted husband had abused her and forced her into prostitution. Understandably, she became so depressed she wanted to take her own life. On the day she had decided to commit suicide, she happened to catch a glimpse of one of this ministry's programs on television. The message of the program—the new life and hope offered in Jesus Christ—captured her attention and led her to put her faith in Christ. Her life was transformed. She found safety and started a new life.

What I came to discover as I attended these meetings was that the power of the ministry wasn't just the result of creating great television that could command a mass audience. Nor was it merely the impact of using powerful new media and technology. When I saw a Coptic Orthodox Archbishop celebrating communion with the Armenian Orthodox Archbishop of Tehran and an Anglican church leader, along with many others from a broad spectrum of the Church of Jesus Christ, I saw why the ministry was having such an impact. I began to understand that by operating as an interdenominational, international coalition, it was realizing Jesus' vision for his Church in relation to bringing the gospel to the world. Just before his crucifixion, Jesus gathered his disciples to present his Last Discourse (John 13–17). Here Jesus outlines how he wants his Church to carry out the Great Commission—together as the Body of Christ. More about this later.

I began to realize God could do in Khorastan what he was doing throughout the Middle East through a coalition-based ministry. In this model, different Christian denominations put aside secondary differences out of their love for Christ to carry out the Great Commission together. I began sharing the vision for developing a coalition-based media ministry for Khorastan. I had no idea how it would happen, but I felt compelled to share the vision with the mission board, denomination leaders, friends, my home church, and anyone who would listen. In 2014, I presented the vision to a broad spectrum of national church leaders in Khorastan, who enthusiastically embraced the idea. We followed up that first consultation with a second one to agree on the values and terms of partnership for the ministry.

One day I received a prayer letter from a Muslim-background evangelist who was doing evangelism and discipleship from Norway as he had been forced out of Khorastan by death threats from radicals. He mentioned he needed a professional camera to produce his videos, and I owned two of the recently developed "mirrorless" professional cameras. Someone could easily film himself using one of these cameras controlled by an app on an iPad. It was perfect for his small one-man studio.

Another Muslim-background believer who was involved in evangelism, leadership training, and church planting from Europe came with me to meet this brother and take the camera to him.

On the Sunday we were there, an unusual thing happened. We went to his local Norwegian church to worship together, and they happened to have a visiting Pentecostal pastor preaching. After the worship time, he called me up for prayer and pronounced a word over me: "[This media effort] will gain momentum, the right leaders will come in, and it will be fruitful."

And this is exactly what began to happen. The ministry has grown to include representatives of a number of branches of the Church, indigenous teams in Khorastan, teams in the UK and the US, and several offices and television studios in country. Gifted leaders, such as my pastor and a senior executive leader from SAT-7, the coalition-based media ministry for the Middle East, joined the effort. Other excellent leaders have joined the boards, the leadership team, and the staff. Millions of people who previously had no chance of ever hearing about the only way of salvation are now hearing about Jesus and the gospel through social media and satellite television.

They are beginning to believe, to follow Christ, and join underground churches. Honestly, I can only marvel that God can use even me in his mission. Believe me, you would marvel too if you knew the pitiful, ruined state I was in before Jesus Christ came into my life. You would also realize if God can use me, he can use anyone who is simply willing.

I believe he wants to use you and my aim is to show you fresh and significant ways he might use you in the greatest of all enterprises—the mission of God. Jesus makes and keeps this promise to his followers: "Truly, truly, I say to you, whoever believes in me will also do the works that I do; and greater works than these will he do, because I am going to the Father" (John 14:12).

Interspersed in the argument for embracing Jesus' vision for his mission are inspiring case studies of "tentmakers," people who are using their vocations to advance God's kingdom. After the conclusion, there are appendices with equipping resources for churches that want to become more missional and for tentmakers who may lack access to traditional resources such as seminaries.

Prologue
The Jonah Paradigm

Contrary to what many of us learned in Sunday School, the Book of Jonah is not about a man who was swallowed by a whale. You may remember how this Jewish prophet tried to dodge God's instruction to go to Nineveh. And honestly, I can't blame him!

Nineveh, the Assyrian capital, was the largest city in the world at that time. It was located in modern-day Mosul, Iraq. The Assyrians were bitter enemies of Israel, and their cruelty and wickedness were legendary. In fact, Assyrian art contains some of the most horrifying images ever created. Their panels depict prisoners having their tongues ripped from their mouths to mute their screams when they were skinned alive. So, it's no wonder Jonah was a bit reluctant to visit these bitter enemies of Israel to call them out on their sins. Imagine how we might feel if God called us to go to an ISIS camp to pronounce God's judgment on them. Besides, God had often warned Israel not to mix with the pagan peoples lest they become like them and start worshipping their false gods.

Instead of going to Nineveh, Jonah sets out in the opposite direction by sea for a distant land, Tarshish, to try to escape the presence of the Lord. Who wouldn't prefer to go to the sunny shores of a prosperous Mediterranean seaside town? But the Lord then sent a great storm. The terrified sailors cried out to their gods for help and cast lots to see why this evil had come upon them.

They already suspected Jonah was the cause of their troubles because he had told them he was fleeing the presence of God. The lot fell to Jonah. After they cast him overboard, God sent a great fish to swallow him.

There has been a lot of speculation about the kind of great fish or whale that might have swallowed him. Here is the truth about the fish: it was actually a "red herring." In other words, the particular type of sea creature is completely irrelevant to the point of our story.

> In the belly of the great fish, Jonah turns to God
> I called out to the Lord, out of my distress,
>   and he answered me;
> out of the belly of Sheol I cried,
>   and you heard my voice. (Jonah 2:1–2)

And here he has a change of heart:

> But I with the voice of thanksgiving
>   will sacrifice to you;
> what I have vowed I will pay.
>   Salvation belongs to the Lord! (2:9)

In the depths, a transformation begins. The great fish vomits Jonah onto the dry land, and again the word of the Lord comes to Jonah, calling him to cry out against Nineveh. This time, however, he obeys, and Nineveh, a bit surprisingly, believes God and repents in sackcloth and ashes.

When God saw they turned away from evil, he relented from destroying the city. But this displeased Jonah greatly:

> "O Lord, is not this what I said when I was yet in my country? That is why I made haste to flee to Tarshish; for I knew that you are a gracious God and merciful, slow to anger and abounding in steadfast love, and relenting from disaster. Therefore now, O Lord, please take my life from me, for it is better for me to die than to live." (4:2–3)

And after the plant that was shading him was destroyed, he became even more angry and depressed.

God draws him out about his anger:

> But God said to Jonah, "Do you do well to be angry for the plant?" And he said, "Yes, I do well to be angry, angry enough to die." And the Lord said, "You pity the plant, for which you did not labor, nor did you make it grow, which came into being in a night and perished in a night. And should not I pity Nineveh, that great city, in which there are more than 120,000 persons who do not know their right hand from their left, and also much cattle?" (4:8–11)

No, Jonah is not a story about a man who was swallowed by a whale. It is a prophetic word to us today. Wouldn't we also be beside ourselves if we suddenly lost our homes? Why then should we not also be concerned for the countless millions who may forever lose any chance of having a heavenly home? The Son of Man had no place to lay his head here, so that we might have a home in heaven.

God might well say to us, "And should I not have compassion on the two billion persons who do not know their right hand from their left?" As Tim Keller suggested, the father's pleading here is much like that of the father of the prodigal son who pleads with the elder son, "It was fitting to celebrate and be glad, for this your brother was dead, and is alive; he was lost, and is found." (Luke 15:32)[1] Here God reveals his heart of love and compassion for a lost and ruined humanity, and his gentleness in dealing with his sometimes clueless Church.

The Book of Jonah is a mirror. When we hold it up, we see ourselves in relation to the Great Commission. God has done great and marvelous things to advance his kingdom in the two thousand years since Christ gave us his Great Commission. He has done so mostly through a relatively small number of dedicated missionaries. But many of the rest of us—at times, myself included—have been all too much like Jonah, not just reluctant prophets but prodigal prophets. But like Jonah, God also subdues us with his love and transforms us by his grace so that we might become instruments of transformation for others who are still lost.

The miracle here is not that Jonah was swallowed by a whale and lived to tell about it. It is that the Father deals with our failure to carry out our assigned task in such a gentle yet pointed way. In the belly of the great fish, Jonah came to the deep transformative realizations about himself and about the wondrous God who had called him. Here he came to realize he was no different than the rebellious Ninevites apart from the Father's grace. And here he came to realize just how gracious and merciful God was. What he had known before about God as an article of faith now becomes something he realizes in his heart. It is in the crucible of suffering rather than the classroom that we learn the deep things of God—the things that transform us and motivate us to obedience regardless of the cost. The belly of the great fish was Jonah's crucible.

God deals with us in the same way he intends to deal with the lost. He brings us to his Kingdom by winning us, not by forcing us. To be sure, he is insistent and firm, and his ways are far above our ways; but above all, he is loving, merciful, and compassionate. He is willing to go to extreme lengths to save us—and many from all nations—from the just wrath that must surely come. He sometimes prods us along with gentle humor, careful not to alienate us even when we, like the world, turn our own back on him. How, then, can we not yield to such a gracious and merciful Father and, in the end, do what he asks us to do?

Beneath the satirical humor lies a profound universal truth. Jonah, though a prophet of God, was no different than those God sent him to redeem, both rebellious sinners in desperate need of a Savior. The cry and confession of both Jonah and the Ninevites is the same: "I called out to the Lord, out of my distress, and he answered me; out of the belly of Sheol I cried, and you heard my voice. Salvation belongs to the Lord!" (2:1–9).

So what does Jonah have to do with the Great Commission and the Church's response to it? *Everything.* It points to the reason for the serious problem in missions. The story of Jonah is what theologians call an "intrusion," a foreshadowing of the Church-age mission inserted into the story of ancient Israel. The norm for Israel in the Old Testament was to avoid dealings with the pagan nations around them. But this event anticipates and looks ahead to the mission of God's people in the

Church Age to come. Throughout the Church Age, we, the Church have often been much like Jonah, a prodigal prophet. As a result, the number of unreached continues to increase over time. And it will increase even more unless there is a radical change in how the Church approaches God's mission.

But God himself has already provided the answer: Jesus Christ's vision for carrying out his mission. The answer has been there all along in the Last Discourse as recorded in the Gospel of John, chapters 13–17. And he has placed it there for us to recover and follow in his time.

PART ONE

THE PROBLEM: THE NUMBER OF UNREACHED IS INCREASING

Chapter 1

The Number of Unreached is Increasing

Why has no one ever told us about this before?
—Afghan man, after hearing the gospel

My first mission trip to Khorastan many years ago left an indelible impression on me. I went with a team to do relief work with the many refugees living in camps there.

One day I went down to the English-language bookstore in the bazaar and asked the clerk to see a Bible. To my astonishment, he had never even heard of the Bible! And yet, there was a huge Pepsi Cola sign in the middle of town; everyone knew what Pepsi was, and probably many, if not most, drank it. As a fairly new believer, I wondered how, two thousand years after God in the flesh had commanded his Church to do this one thing, bring the gospel to all nations, there were still so many places on earth where almost no one had even heard of the Bible. This question has haunted me ever since, and it is only now, some forty years later, that I have come to understand how and why this could happen and, more importantly, how the situation can be rectified. That's what this book is about.

It is a great marvel that Almighty God has chosen, as his junior partner in his mission, the fallen humanity he set out to redeem. That God created this vast and beautiful creation out of nothing is astounding; that he does the greater work of redeeming all nations through a partnership with such a humble and fallible partner is even more amazing.

Consider how great God's work of creation is: the known universe has two trillion galaxies, each with 100 billion stars, not to mention the wonders of life on the earth. The beauty and complexity of God's creation are mind-boggling. But consider how much greater God's redemptive work is. He produced his creation out of nothing, but in his work of redemption, he accomplished a far greater feat. For one thing, accomplishing our redemption cost him his Son. And in applying that redemption, he began not from scratch, but with a humanity so ruined by sin that it hated him and stood in blind and bitter rebellion against him. He began by calling some from among those utterly ruined by sin to participate with himself as a sort of "junior partner" in making that redemption known. Consider the state of humanity before God called Abram to begin the process of preparing the world for the redemption to come:

> The Lord saw that the wickedness of man was great in the earth, and that every intention of the thoughts of his heart was only evil continually. And the Lord regretted

that he had made man on the earth, and it grieved him to his heart. (Genesis 6:5–6)

Exactly as Jesus taught, the growth of the Kingdom of God has been like that of a mustard seed. The smallest seed in the garden has become the greatest tree in the garden. The Church, in the broadest sense of "all God's called-out people," has grown from that one man, Abram, who believed God four thousand years ago to become the largest global organization in the world by far, numbering 2.7 billion. The Church is present in each of the 195 countries in the world, even where conversion to Christ is punishable by death. This growth has been both astonishing and unparalleled.

Much significant church growth has occurred in the past seventy-five years, often in the face of the most severe repression and persecution. China had only about three million Christians at the time of the Communist Revolution in 1949, when the new government expelled all the missionaries. Years of severe persecution followed in a relentless effort to eradicate the faith. According to the Joshua Project, the result has been the most explosive church growth in history, resulting in some one hundred million having come to faith in China as of 2025.

A similar story of God's triumph over the best efforts of those who oppose the gospel has played out in Iran. At the time of the revolution in 1979, there were only about five hundred Iranian Christians from a Muslim background. Again the missionaries were expelled, and that marked the start of a period of explosive evangelical church growth, now at a rate of approximately 19.6% as of 2024.[2] Today there are approximately one million believers from a majority Muslim background in Iran.

Again, a similar story is playing out in Afghanistan. In 1952, when pioneer modern missionary J. Christy Wilson first went to Kabul, there were no known Muslim-background believers. Radicals resisted, and in 1973 destroyed the church pastored by Dr. Wilson, the Kabul Community Church, and Dr. Wilson was forced to flee after a plot to murder him came to light. Today, the number of underground believers is in the thousands.

God has brought these and many other amazing advances, typically through the dedicated work of a relatively small number of career missionaries who have poured out their lives for the sake of Christ and the gospel. And since the 1970's, radio and subsequently satellite television and social media have fueled significant church growth, especially in countries closed to conventional missions.

In spite of the many other remarkable advances of the gospel worldwide, there remains a massive, urgent problem in the world of missions. Between 1900 and 2000, the number of unreached peoples increased by 969 million. More troubling, without a radical change in the trend, between 2000 and 2050, the number of unreached is projected to increase by another 923 million to a total of 2.772 billion.[3]

This means that countless millions will live and die without ever having had a chance to hear of the only way of salvation unless there is a change in how we carry out the Great Commission.

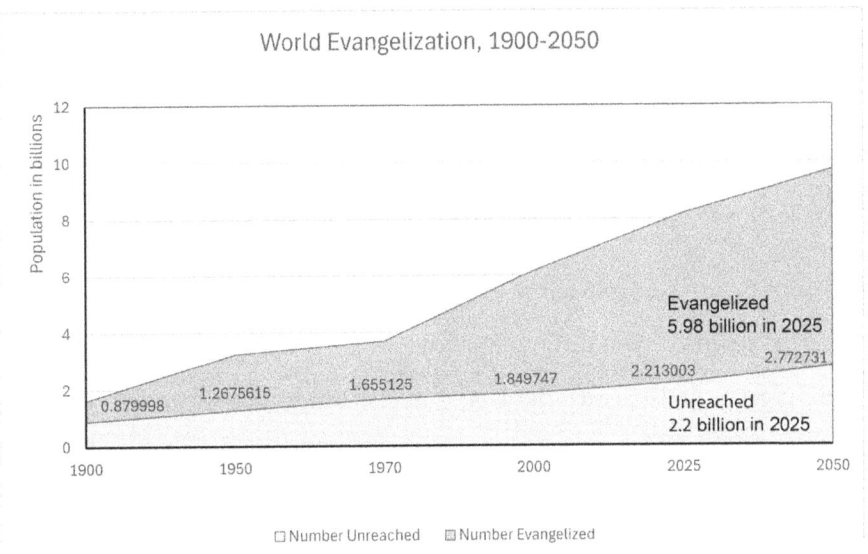

The above graph showing 2.2 billion unreached peoples as of 2025 gives the most conservative number, and refers only to people with no access to the gospel.[4] Using the broader, more common definition of "unreached people groups," i.e., those with 2% or fewer Evangelical Christians, yields the number of 3.42 billion as of 2025, according to the Joshua Project.[5] Regardless of which figure is used, the number is alarmingly high.

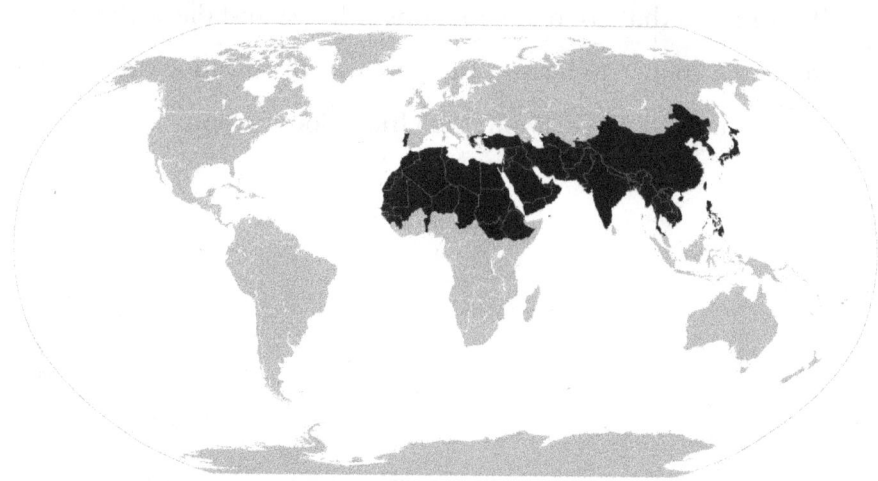

For clarity, "people groups" are groups which share a common language, culture, and identity. Those which are "unreached" have little or no access to the gospel. Generally, these groups have fewer than 2% Evangelical Christians. Most of these groups live in the "10/40 Window," the area on the map between the 10- and 40-degree north latitude lines. This area runs from North Africa to East Asia. See the above map.

Questions for Reflection and Discussion

These questions can be used for personal reflection or small group discussion:

1. Do you think most Christians know that the number of unreached people is increasing?

2. Why do you think this number continues to rise?

3. What can you or your church do to help address this issue?

Chapter 2

Why the Number of Unreached is Increasing

We've strayed from being fishers of men to being keepers of the aquarium.
—Paul Harvey

I have already mentioned how on my first trip to Khorastan, I was amazed to discover that almost no one had ever heard of the only way of salvation. What I didn't realize at the time was that this was just the tip of the iceberg. Over time, I came to realize that countless millions have never heard, and I came to realize why.

There are six main reasons the number of unreached is increasing. First, most churchgoers are not engaged in carrying out the Great Commission. Second, the vast majority of church personnel and resources are devoted to populations that already have access to the gospel. Third, the Church is not immune to a kind of conflict of interest that economists call "the principal-agency problem." This conflict of interest arises when one person delegates a task to another. Fourth, the Church often gets enmeshed in and sidetracked by politics. And fifth, the world, the flesh, and the devil relentlessly oppose the advance of God's Kingdom. Finally, few Christians are carrying out the Great Commission the way Jesus has prescribed.

The great paradox of the Christian faith is that even though the "grand narrative" of the Bible is the mission of God, and even though Jesus entrusted carrying out his Great Commission as the Church's primary task, missions has been marginalized or ignored throughout church history, according to noted missionary and researcher Patrick Johnstone.[6] The fact that we have a special category of Christians whose distinctive is carrying out the Great Commission (i.e., "Evangelicals") is in itself telling; that in itself reveals evangelism is not normative for most Christians.

MOST CHURCHGOERS ARE NOT ENGAGED IN THE MISSION OF THE CHURCH

How do we know most churchgoers are not meaningfully engaged in carrying out the Great Commission? A recent Barna survey revealed that the majority of church attenders in the US either don't know what the Great Commission is or are unable to say what it is.[7]

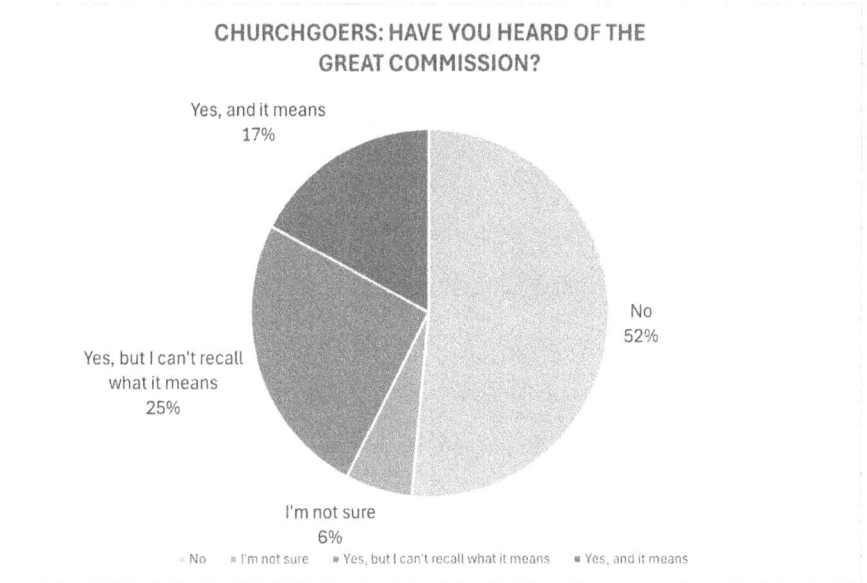

Source: barna.com

From the 2018 Barna survey, 51% of churchgoers say they have never heard of the Great Commission and another 25% can't recall what it is exactly. And if the majority of churchgoers don't know what the Church's mission is, how can they be meaningfully engaged in helping to carry it out?

This unfamiliarity with the Great Commission in the US Church is mirrored in the global Church.

According to the 2024 Lausanne Movement's *State of the Great Commission Report*:

> The majority of the 1,500 global Christian leaders surveyed believe that less than half of the Christians in their region would be able to say what the Great Commission is.[8]

Very Few Church Personnel and Resources Devoted to Reaching the Unreached

The number of unreached is also increasing because most of the church personnel and resources are devoted to work among populations that already have access to the gospel. Some 70% of Evangelicals are unaware that there are still many millions of unevangelized people in the world.[9] The graph below shows that only about 3 percent of church workers serve the least reached.[10]

In addition, only about one-tenth of 1 percent of global Christian giving is allocated to support missions to the unreached. It is shocking to consider that only about $1.4 billion[11] [12] is given to reach the unreached yearly compared to $1,304 billion in total Christian giving.[13] The amount given to reach the unreached yearly is only

.002% of Christians' yearly income of $70 trillion as of 2024.[14] The yearly amount given to reach the unreached constitutes only .000869% of the $161.751 trillion owned by Christians.[15]

To be clear, it is not as though simply increasing the amount of money given to missions would, in itself, advance God's kingdom; it would not. The lack of giving to missions is more of a symptom of the deeper problem rather than a cause. As the late Senate Chaplain Richard Halverson put it, "Jesus Christ said more about money than about any other single thing because, when it comes to a man's real nature, money is of first importance. Money is an exact index to a man's character."[16] The real problem in relation to the relative lack of strategic giving to Christ's mission is in what it may reveal about our hearts, or at least our lack of knowledge.

Case Study: Mohamad, Iranian Minister of the Gospel

Mohamad is the author of *Forsaking My Father's Religion* and president of Iranian Christians International. He was a zealous Shiite Muslim until he came to faith in Jesus Christ through a friend's testimony in 1999.

How did you come to faith in Christ?

I was born and raised in a poor, devout Shiite family in Tehran, Iran. My father came from Northern Iran and worked as a lab technician. My mother came from a very religious Muslim family. She worked as a phone operator in the hospital until she got married. After that, she stayed at home and took care of me and my two older brothers.

All children born into a Muslim family are dedicated to Islam at birth by the reciting of the Shahada ("There is no god but God, and Mohammad is his messenger") in their ears before being handed to their mother. It was no different for me. From a young age, I learned to read and recite the Quran, the holy book of Islam, in Arabic, even though my mother tongue was Farsi. My parents insisted that I participate in the various Shiite rituals, and that I attend congregational prayer and Quran classes in the Mosque. I was taught and confessed, "There is no god but Allah and Muhammad is his prophet."

I was also taught, along with all other Muslim children, that Islam is the culmination of all religions and superior to all other ways of life. Allah and his prophet Muhammad, who is Allah's last messenger, wish to see Islam established throughout the world.

From a young age, I ached to know Allah and loved learning about Islam. Islam is a religion of submission; the word Islam literally means submission and surrender. I willingly surrendered myself to the submission of Islam. As a result, I joined religious groups and became the most zealous of my family in seeking Allah and in following Islam.

During the month of Ramadan, I fasted for thirty days and recited the Quran. The following month in the Shiite calendar is a month of blood, in which we would mourn for the dead Imams. During the times of mourning, we would gather at certain shrines and weep and cut and beat ourselves to show our devotion. Blood would run down my head as I imitated the way Imam Ali was martyred. It was our duty to wait for the return of the twelfth Imam, and I zealously prayed for this, but it never happened. I was taught the only certain way to enter Paradise was to become a martyr in a holy war or Jihad.

When I was twenty-two, I completed my mandatory service with the Iranian Revolutionary Guard. Soon after that, I met with an old high school friend to catch up. He told me about how his life had been transformed for the better. He said that Jesus Christ had sacrificed himself and suffered for the forgiveness of our sins. He was rejected, bruised, beaten, and nailed to a cross for our forgiveness. This was the very thing I had sought through my own suffering. I now realized that it was the suffering of Christ on the cross that would give me the eternal life I sought. It brought me to my knees. I repented of my sins and gave my life to Christ on the spot.

How did you become a minister of the Gospel?

After I converted, I attended an Armenian Iranian Church that had a Pakistani pastor. The pastor began to disciple me. I worked as a taxi driver, and I would listen to an audio Bible. I kept a Bible on the dashboard, and whenever a passenger would ask me about it, I would tell them about Jesus. Some came to faith, but others rejected the message. Eventually, the owner of the company took me aside and said some of the passengers had reported me to the Iranian government.

At first, I thought I could just move to a different city in Iran, but the Christians there told me it was too dangerous as they, too, were under pressure. I ended up buying a bus ticket to Turkey, leaving

> behind everyone I knew and everything I owned. In Turkey, I endured a lot of discrimination and difficulty as I waited for the UN to adjudicate my asylum case. I was given the most menial and physically demanding work.
>
> After a long, difficult time in Turkey as a refugee, I was finally accepted to come to America. I felt God's call to ministry and attended Bible college, graduating in 2019 and becoming president of Iranian Christians International.

THE "PRINCIPAL-AGENCY PROBLEM" IN THE CHURCH'S STEWARDSHIP

Do you remember Jesus' parable of the talents? The master entrusted his property to his servants: one received five, one received two, and another received only one. The first two servants multiplied the talents entrusted to them, and when the master returned, he commended them, and the master set them over much.

But the third servant was afraid and buried his talent. When confronted, this servant said, "Master, I knew you to be a hard man, reaping where you did not sow, and gathering where you scattered no seed, so I was afraid, and I went and hid your talent in the ground" (Matthew 25:24,25). But the master condemned that servant as wicked and slothful and gave his talent to the one who had ten.

Here we can see the disastrous result not only of bad theology ("I knew you to be a hard man . . .") but also of acting on the basis of fear and perceived self-interest rather than on the basis of really knowing and trusting the all-sufficient God of love. A similar kind of problem occurs in the Parable of the Tenants (Matthew 21:33–41).

Economists speak of the "principal-agency problem," which is the conflict of interest inherent whenever a principal entrusts the management of his affairs to an agent, who is supposed to act on behalf of the principal and to maximize results for the benefit of that principal.[17]

This kind of conflict of interest would come into play when, for example, someone (the principal) hires a money manager (the agent) to manage his retirement account. Even though the highest returns will result from buying and holding stocks in high-quality companies over the long term, his broker might engage in frequent trading in the short term in order to generate commissions for himself at the expense of long-term gains for his principal. The broker's self-serving impairs his ability to serve the interests of his client.

God has entrusted the Church with his mission and the responsibility of bringing the Good News of his redemption to all nations during the Church Age. God is the "principal," and the Church is the "agent." However, much like Jonah, we are often more aware of and concerned about our own needs rather than the need to extend God's Kingdom to all nations.

The Church is not immune to the temptation of this kind of common conflict of interest. For example, a church board (the agent) may face a similar situation when it is called upon to decide whether to spend the Lord's funds to benefit the local congregation or to serve the needs of a mission to the unreached. I am grateful that God is stirring a deep level of engagement in his mission at the church we are privileged to be part of. It is reflected in an emerging giving pattern: in 2024 this medium-sized congregation gave just under $700,000 to support missions compared to $1,000,000 given to the general fund, according to the final budget figures. This church is recovering a radical generosity and a lively engagement in the Lord's mission. We are beginning to see a resurgence of mission engagement as part of our identity as Christians. This giving pattern reflects the congregation's love for Christ and desire to give themselves to the task he has entrusted to us. It reflects the very heart of God for his lost sheep. This was also the Apostle Paul's heart; he said, "It has always been my ambition to preach the gospel where Christ was not known" (Romans 15:20, NIV).

The principle-agency problem may not necessarily be the result of malicious intent. It may simply result from the fact that we naturally think about our own needs or the needs of those we are aware of before we consider the needs of those who live ten thousand miles away. We may not even know they exist, much less be aware of the distant need. It may result from being part of a church in which the Great Commission has not been preached, taught, or practiced. Missions just might not be part of the church's culture. That can change. See Appendix G, Ten Ways to Become a More Missional Church, for a helpful resource to assist local churches in becoming more missional.

Regardless of the cause, this conflict of interest is one of the reasons that the mission of the church is often marginalized.

The Politicization of the Church

The advance of the gospel in the Roman Empire slowed after the Christian faith became the religion of the establishment with the conversion of Emperor Constantine in 312. This example of church-state entanglement is not unique. Other examples include that of Vladimir the Great of the early Russian state, who in 986 sent envoys throughout the world to consider the various options for a state religion: Latin Christianity, Judaism, and Byzantine Christianity. They were most impressed by their visit to Constantinople:

> We know not whether we were in Heaven or on Earth.... We only know that God dwells there among the people, and their service is fairer than the ceremonies of other nations.[18]

Initially, Vladimir rejected the various options except for the Eastern Orthodox rite, yet stopped short of converting. But he eventually agreed to convert and Christianize his people as part of an agreement to wed Anna, sister of Byzantine Emperor Basil II.[19]

This close relationship between the Russian Orthodox Church and the Russian state has continued over time. According to Soviet archives, its billionaire patriarch was a KGB officer; he remains a close ally of Vladimir Putin, the former director of the FSB (the successor agency of the KGB).[20] This relationship may help explain why in 2022, he reportedly promised Russian soldiers that if they died in the war against Ukraine, "this sacrifice washes away all their sins."[21]

If such reports are correct, it suggests a political influence over that church which is antithetical to the mission of the Church. Along with Russia's invasion of Ukraine, there have been over thirty cases of non-Orthodox clergy being kidnapped or murdered, and over a hundred cases of interrogations, expulsions, and imprisonments by Russian state actors. In addition, some six hundred houses of worship have been destroyed in what some are calling "Russia's war against evangelicals."[22] Needless to say, such a church-state partnership does not advance God's Kingdom; it does the exact opposite.

The situation is Russia is not unique. This example of church-state entanglements is not merely an interesting case study. It is a serious cautionary tale for the Church in every nation. Rather than assuming "it can't happen here," we should heed the scriptural warnings and calls to discernment and endurance during the Church Age.

The Lord calls some Christians to be salt and light in the political realm, but they must be "wise as serpents and gentle as doves." There are several political pitfalls that divert the Church from her mission, especially during the "last days," the troubled period that began at Pentecost (Acts 2:17, 2 Tim. 3:1–5). One is partnering with unbelievers, as in the case of Russia. A related pitfall is the mistaken belief that political action can replace evangelism. And a third is allowing a political philosophy or party to give us our sense of identity, values, and purpose. These are things God alone can give the believer.

Clearly, Jesus said, "My kingdom is not of this world" (John 18:36). Therefore, his Church must not be come under any political authority and must avoid all compromising political entanglements. This is especially critical in troubled times. This fallen world is enemy territory, if we take the Bible seriously. The spirit, principles, belief systems, methods, and ends of worldly politics and those of the Christian faith are ultimately incompatible. For example, the world often operates on the principles of self-interest, deception, force, and fear, but the Kingdom of God operates on the principles of love, revelation, attraction, and faith. Compromising entanglements of the Church in politics serve as sad reminders that adding the imperfect to the perfect produces the imperfect. God is not redeeming the world; he is redeeming a people for himself out of the world into his Kingdom.

Rather than partnering and compromising with the world, noted missiologist Patrick Johnstone suggests following the way of the cross over the way of the world. He says, "The solution is not a Christian political take-over of nations—which has had a very negative history and is a discredit to the Gospel."[23]

When the chief priests and Pharisees came with torches and weapons to arrest Jesus, he resigned himself to the Father's will. But Peter jumped to his defense, striking the high priest's servant and severing his ear. To Peter, this seemed like the obvious thing to do. But Jesus corrected him and told him to sheath his sword. Peter did not yet comprehend that the mission of God is far above the petty power plays of this world.

He said, "Shall I not drink the cup that the Father has given me?" (Matthew 18:11). Jesus' kingdom is not of this world, and Peter's action didn't advance the mission of God; it could have short-circuited it. As James said, "Do you not know that friendship with the world is enmity with God? Therefore whoever wishes to be a friend of the world makes himself an enemy of God" (James 4:4). For this reason, the political arena can be just as lethal to the modern Christian as the Roman arena was to the early Christian. It can be even more dangerous because often, the danger isn't perceived. Politics can divert believers from God's eternal purposes into merely temporal purposes with no eternal value.

There is a larger context for the politicization of the Church. The Church can become vulnerable to selling her sacred birthright for a mess of political pottage when she is unsure of the rock-solid foundation of the knowledge of God. Pastor John Piper puts it this way:

> The strong timber of the tree of evangelicalism has historically been the great doctrines of the Bible:
> - God's glorious perfections
> - man's fallen nature
> - the wonders of redemptive history
> - the magnificent work of redemption in Christ
> - the saving and sanctifying work of grace in the soul
> - the great mission of the church in conflict with the world, the flesh, and the devil
> - the greatness of our hope of everlasting joy at God's right hand
>
> These unspeakably magnificent things once defined us and were the strong timber and root supporting the fragile leaves and fruit of our religious affections and moral actions. But this is not the case for many churches and denominations and ministries and movements in Evangelicalism today. And that is why the waving leaves of present evangelical success and the sweet fruit of prosperity are not as promising as we may think. There is a hollowness to this triumph, and the tree is weak even while the leafy branches are waving in the sun.
>
> What is missing is the mind-shaping knowledge and the all-transforming enjoyment of the weight of the glory of God. The glory of God—holy, righteous, all-sovereign, all-wise, all-good—is missing. God rests lightly on the church in America. He is not felt as a weighty concern. Wells puts it starkly: "It is this God, majestic and holy in

his being, this God whose love knows no bounds because his holiness knows no limits, who has disappeared from the modern evangelical world." It is an overstatement. But not without warrant.[24]

When we don't see Christ's glory clearly, we can become more vulnerable to the sway of lesser lights.

How are we to understand and deal with the turmoil of the Church Age? How are we to understand the purposes of God when we see the political turmoil, natural disasters, wars, famines, and earthquakes Jesus foretold? These things can shake us from our comfortable places.

I once heard about a lumberjack who was sent to clear an entire forest. While felling some trees, he noticed a robin building her nest in one of the trees. Not wanting to destroy her home, the lumberjack pounded on the tree until the robin flew away to another tree. Again, he pounded and shook the tree until she fled. He did the same every time she tried to build her nest in a tree. Finally, she gave up and fled to a rock, where she safely built her nest.

God uses the disasters and turmoil of this world in a similar way. He doesn't want us to build our lives upon the sinking sand of a fallen world that is passing away; he wants us to find our home on the rock that never fails. We naturally seek a comfortable home in the world, but God is committed to seeing us securely settled on the rock.

Using such symbols as "Babylon" (Revelation 17:5), the book of Revelation reveals that there is something much more sinister behind the world's seductions, persecutions, and lawlessness, which can deflect Christians from Christ and the gospel: the spiritual powers of darkness (2 Thess. 2:3–12, 1 John 2:18).

The Invisible Cosmic Spiritual War That Rages

William Tyndale is a familiar name in most of the English-speaking world, but few people today know his fascinating story. Tyndale was a Bible scholar who lived in the 1500s. He was the first to translate the Bible into English from the original languages and inspired the translations that followed, such as the King James Version.

His English New Testament was published in Germany in 1526 and smuggled from Europe into England and Scotland. The religious establishment of the day condemned him as a heretic and banned his New Testament, burning all available copies.[25]

What were his alleged offenses?

- First, he had maintained that faith alone justifies.
- Second, he maintained that to believe in the forgiveness of sins and to embrace the mercy offered in the gospel was enough for salvation.
- Third, he averred that human traditions cannot bind the conscience, except where their neglect might occasion scandal . . .[26]

Tyndale was strangled and his body burned at the stake for believing the gospel and making it freely available.

These kinds of events seem incomprehensible to the modern mind, especially in the free countries of the Western world. But it is instructive to consider why such cruel and violent reactions against the gospel and those that make it known have happened over and over in history.

These things are surprising only if we don't take what the Bible plainly teaches about the devil, the world, and the flesh seriously. By "the world," I don't mean the created world, but rather the corrupt system that now operates in this world. And by "the flesh," I don't mean the body, but rather the fallen condition we find ourselves in apart from the grace of God.

The Kingdom of God and the Kingdom of Darkness are locked in a cosmic death struggle. The fallen, fallible, limited, and doomed powers of darkness know they can never win against the Almighty, all-knowing, sovereign Lord. They know their doom is sure. Their only hope is to try to prolong the period before they face the inevitable final judgment, the fierce wrath of God, and their eternal punishment. They also know that the gospel of the Kingdom must be preached in all nations before the final judgment comes (Matthew 24:14). Therefore, the highest priority strategic focus of their efforts is against the gospel and against the propagation of the gospel to all nations. Only by trying to "run out the clock" and delay the evangelization of the world can they have any hope of delaying the inevitable fierce and just wrath of the Holy Almighty God they have defied.

It therefore stands to reason that the Kingdom of Darkness would seek these strategic goals:

1. Undermine confidence in the authority of the Bible since it is God's unique written revelation

2. Divide the Church since a unified Church is necessary for world evangelization and a house divided cannot stand

3. Obscure the gospel of grace since it signals the conquest of evil (Matthew 24:14)

4. Marginalize the mission of the Church since world evangelization signals the end of the Kingdom of Darkness

5. Obscure the fact that mission engagement is a part of following Christ because that greatly impedes world evangelization

The powers of darkness deceive the mind, seduce the heart, and enslave the will through false narratives and idols. In the modern world, popular idols are more apt to be abstract ideas and ideologies than the statues of antiquity. But they still falsely promise happiness if we will only worship money, power, pleasure, fame, demagogues, or the gods of false religions. We are worshippers by design and nature, and if we don't worship the living God who alone can satisfy our hearts, we must inevitably worship some worthless and enslaving substitute. This is how most spiritual warfare is conducted.

We see this hidden spiritual dynamic of spiritual warfare in church history. It is part of the underlying reason the gospel itself was almost lost for a time prior to the Reformation; people commonly thought they could save themselves by their own efforts. This spiritual warfare is also a significant reason the mission of the Church has been marginalized and neglected through much of Church history, and most obviously prior to the modern Protestant Missions movement of the eighteenth century. And it is one of the underlying reasons that the mission is not part of the identity of most Christians.

If the biblical worldview is correct, we would expect that over time, absent God's gracious intervention, spiritual decline would occur in institutions. This pattern recurs frequently in the Old Testament. Israel continued to fall back into unbelief, rebellion, and idolatry. The human condition is not morally neutral. Apart from God's redeeming, sustaining, and renewing grace, the devil, the world, and the flesh will exert an inexorable gravitational pull downward and backward. This is why revival, renewal, and reformation are desperately needed and have been graciously granted throughout history.

This gravitational pull draws people away from the purposes of God. They may be subtly diverted from the best purposes to merely good purposes, rather than to purposes of obvious evil. But the effect in relation to forsaking the purposes of God is the same.

Given that Satan is the god and ruler of this world who has the power to blind the minds of people (2 Corinthians 4:4, I John 5:19, John 14:30), the invisible work of the Kingdom of Darkness is a major underlying cause of the neglect of the church's mission. The fact that so many people would be quick to ignore or dismiss this cause without considering it simply illustrates how great this problem is and proves the point.

There is one final reason we have not yet brought the gospel to all nations two thousand years after the Great Commission: Jesus' vision for carrying out his mission has often been overlooked.

Few Christians Are Carrying Out Jesus' Mission According to His Vision and Plan

The question of strategy in missions is essentially a theological problem. In other words, the question is not "What is the best idea we can come up with?" Rather it is "What is Jesus' vision and plan for the fulfillment of his mission?" It is God's mission. Simply doing more of the same will not reverse a long-standing structural problem; only a new paradigm can do that.

Jesus sets out his vision and plan for the Church to carry out the Great Commission and to continue his mission in the Last Discourse as recorded in John chapters 13 to 17. He concludes with a prayer:

> I do not ask for these only, but also for those who will believe in me through their word, that they may all be one, just as you, Father, are in me, and I in you, that they also may be in us, so that the world may believe that you have sent me. (John 17: 20–21)

Essentially, Jesus prays that his Church might be one so that the world may believe the Father has sent him. This unity implies two things. First, that God intends to bring the gospel to the nations through the Body of Christ, not just through the relatively small number of professional missionaries alone. Second, the request "that they may *all* be one" [italics added] implies that every Christian can be and ought to be part of this effort. Jesus' vision as set out in the Last Discourse will be examined more fully in Section 2, but for the moment, it is clear today that few are carrying out the Commission according to Jesus' vision, i.e., as part of an interdenominational coalition with virtually "all hands on deck."

There are a number of reasons that Christians have not been working together in God's mission. **First, prior to the *Joint Declaration on Justification* of 1999, the divided Church could not work together in unity because it could not agree on the essential gospel message.** But in the twenty-first century, such a united witness seems more feasible for the first time since the Reformation now that there is historic agreement that the gospel is a gift of grace. In this historic *Declaration*, the Catholic Church joined the Lutheran World Federation in affirming that Luther's understanding of justification was correct:

> Together we confess: By grace alone, in faith in Christ's saving work and not because of any merit on our part, we are accepted by God and receive the Holy Spirit, who renews our hearts while equipping and calling us to good works.[27] [28]

Second, a united witness has been impossible since most modern Christians don't see engagement in the mission as an essential part of their identity. More about this, as well, in Part Two.

To understand the present predicament of the Church in relation to her mission, it's helpful to consider how the Church came to lose her way in relation to the mission Christ entrusted to her.

QUESTIONS FOR REFLECTION AND DISCUSSION

1. What do you think are the main causes of the increasing number of unreached people?

2. What can you or your church do to help address those issues?

CHAPTER 3

HOW THE CHURCH CAME TO MARGINALIZE HER MISSION EVEN THOUGH THE MISSION OF GOD IS THE BIBLE'S CENTRAL THEME

> The gospel is only good news if it
> gets there in time.
> —CARL F.H. HENRY

ONE DAY AT THE office, two Christian men on a break struck up a conversation about whether or not evangelizing the unreached is a priority. As Jim poured himself some water he said, "It really doesn't matter that much because God is merciful, so he wouldn't condemn someone who never had a chance to hear about Christ."

His friend Paul answered him thoughtfully: "Which is better to rely on: speculative theology or what God says?" Jim answered, "Well if you put it that way, I suppose what God says." Paul then quoted Acts 4:12: "There is salvation in no one else, for there is no other name under heaven given among men by which we must be saved." He added, "Not only that, if all those who have never heard the gospel are automatically saved, doing nothing would then be the perfect way to ensure the salvation of all the unreached. But if that were true, why would Jesus Christ have commanded his Church to bring the gospel to all nations, and why would so many, beginning with the Apostles, have sacrificed their lives to bring the gospel to a lost world?"

Noted missionary leader and author Patrick Johnstone has ably outlined the historical roots of the Church's lapses in relation to world evangelization in his book *The Church is Bigger Than You Think*.[29] The following four factors are drawn heavily from his analysis: the slowness of the disciples to grasp the mission followed by minimizing the mission of the Church in interpretations, theology, and church history.

SLOWNESS OF THE DISCIPLES TO GRASP THEIR MISSION

Consider how slow the disciples were to even grasp who Jesus was:

> Philip said to him, "Lord, show us the Father, and it is enough for us." Jesus said to him, "Have I been with you so long, and you still do not know me, Philip? Whoever has seen me has seen the Father. How can you say, 'Show us the Father'?" (John 14:8–9)

Even though Christ had commanded his disciples to make disciples of "all nations," it was only after the intervention of an angel that the

Italian centurion Cornelius came to faith. Peter himself required a confirming vision, repeated three times, that what God makes clean must not be called common. After the Holy Spirit fell on the Gentiles as Peter preached the gospel to them, "the believers from among the circumcised were amazed, because the gift of the Holy Spirit was poured out even on the Gentiles" (Acts 10:45). When Peter reported back to the church in Jerusalem, he had to argue the case to finally get the Jewish believers to accept the fact that the vision from heaven included the Gentiles: "If then God gave the same gift to them as he gave to us when we believed in the Lord Jesus Christ, who was I that I could stand in God's way?" (Acts 11:17). The Jewish church only reluctantly conceded that the gospel was for all nations.

It was not until the Council of Jerusalem c. 48 AD, some fifteen years after Pentecost, that the issue of the Gentiles would finally be resolved.[30]

Missing the Centrality of God's Mission in Interpreting the Bible

Translations of the Bible also have often downplayed the centrality of God's mission in the way certain key words have been translated. For example, in the Greek New Testament, the essential Great Commission verb *evangelize* (*euangelizo*) appears fifty-six times.[31] However, in the King James Version (KJV) and English Standard Versions (ESV), the word does not appear. Similarly, the words for "mission" and "missionary" never appear in the KJV or ESV translations of the Bible. Even though the word itself does not appear in the

Greek text, the concept is central. See Appendix B, which shows the mission of God is the central theme of the Bible.

The word "apostle" appears eighty (KJV) or ninety (ESV) times. The underlying Greek word *apostolos* occurs eighty times in the New Testament. In general, an apostle is "one who is sent out on a mission." In Church history, it means one who is sent out to be "a witness to the risen Christ and his finished work."[32] Used in this way, once the last eyewitness died, the office of apostle could not continue.[33]

The word "apostle" in the more general sense of "one who is sent out on a mission" has largely fallen into disuse in the mainstream because of the ambiguity of the term. Furthermore, most Protestants don't use the term in relation to missions because they are understandably leery of assigning too much authority to those who would be designated as modern "apostles."

Therefore, it has often been difficult to even find biblical language to talk about the mission, even though the mission of God and its continuation through the work of the Church comprise the central theme of the Bible.

Minimizing God's Mission in Theology

Many of the Christian confessions and creeds were used to clarify Christian truth in relation to heresies and to correct common misunderstandings of scripture. They typically clarified the doctrines about the person and work of Christ as well as the nature of salvation.

Unfortunately, this reactive method led to a major omission. Almost all of the various major confessions and creeds from the first century up to the post-Reformation period do not say a single word about the mission of the Church. An example is the Apostles Creed, the Christian creed most widely read in the church. Here is a sampling of the major creeds and confessions and their treatment of the mission of the Church:

120–250	Apostles' Creed	No mention of the Church's mission
381	Nicene Creed	No mention of the Church's mission
500	Athanasian Creed	No mention of the Church's mission
1563	Heidelberg Confession	No mention of the Church's mission
1566	Belgic Confession	No mention of the Church's mission
1618–19	The Canons of Dort	One mention (Second Point, Article 5)
1992	Catechism of the Catholic Church	One mention (Section Two, Article 3, III)

Even the high-water mark, theologically sound Westminster Shorter Catechism (1646–47) makes mention of praying for the Kingdom, but makes no mention of carrying out the mission of bringing the gospel of the Kingdom to the nations in the answer to Question 102: "What do we pray for in the second petition?" Similarly, the Larger Catechism answer to Question 191 makes a single mention of the church's mission as something to pray for, in explaining the meaning of the second petition: "Thy kingdom come." The Westminster Confession (1646) itself makes no reference to the Church's mission or the Great Commission.[34]

Similarly, the first-century *Didache* ("Teaching"), the oldest extant Christian catechism, makes no mention whatsoever of the mission of the Church.[35]

Patrick Johnstone sums up the profound effects of this theological blind spot: "This astonishing lack of reference to the resurrection ministry of Jesus or the task of the Church for world evangelization is an error of enormous proportions and has distorted theological education to the present day."[36]

MISSING AND MINIMIZING THE GLOBAL MISSION VISION IN CHURCH HISTORY

Some in the Church have been slow to grasp Christ's global mission vision almost from the start. We tend to idealize the early Church because God did such wonderful and amazing things through it. We think of the visitation of the Holy Spirit at Pentecost and the 3000 "devout men from every nation under heaven" (Acts 2:5) and how they received the gospel with repentance and were baptized. Yet the early church leaders and believers were ordinary, fallible human beings, as we all are.

We tend to overlook the fact that the disciples remained in Palestine for at least five to six years before carrying out the command of Jesus to bring the gospel to all nations.[37] Though an apostle is "one who is sent out on a mission," ironically, the apostles still remained in Jerusalem during the persecution of 35–37 AD:

> And there arose on that day a great persecution against the church in Jerusalem, and they were all scattered throughout the regions of Judea and Samaria, except the apostles . . . Now those who were scattered went about preaching the word. Philip went down to the city of Samaria and proclaimed to them the Christ. (Acts 8:1–4)

In this passage, we see it was everyone except the apostles who went about preaching the word beyond Jerusalem. It is easily overlooked that these ordinary Christians, who were scattered as a result of the persecution, took the lead and were the first to carry out the Great Commission beyond Palestine by planting a church cross-culturally beyond Judea and Samaria:

> Now those who were scattered because of the persecution that arose over Stephen traveled as far as Phoenicia and Cyprus and Antioch, speaking the word to no one except Jews. But there were some of them, men of Cyprus and Cyrene, who on coming to Antioch spoke to the Hellenists also, preaching the Lord Jesus. And the hand of the Lord was with them, and a great number who believed turned to the Lord. (Acts 11:19–21)

Even though the Apostles got off to a slow start, it never occurred to these ordinary Christians that they could follow Christ and, at the same time, ignore the commission he gave them. Mission engagement was part of their identity as followers of Christ. And two deacons, Stephen (Acts 7) and Philip (Acts 8:5) first took the initiative to preach the gospel in Palestine at the time of the persecution.

In spite of their slow start, the Apostles amazingly brought the faith to about 30% of the known ancient world within 50 years of the resurrection.[38] Each of the eleven apostles helped bring the gospel to the ancient world from Asia Minor to Persia to India. And, of course, the Apostle Paul preached the gospel and planted the Church throughout the Mediterranean region, including Asia Minor, Greece, Italy, Malta, Crete, Cyprus. All except John would be martyred in the process.

It might be surprising to some modern Christians that the missionary methods of the ancient church differed significantly from those of the of the modern church:

> ... for the ancient church knew nothing of "evangelistic services" or "revivals." On the contrary, in the early church worship centered on communion, and only baptized Christians were admitted to its celebration. Therefore, evangelism did not take place in church services, but rather, as Celsus said, in kitchens, shops, and markets."[39]

As mentioned, when Emperor Constantine embraced the Christian faith in 312 AD, the Christian faith began to change from being a persecuted dynamic outsider movement to an established but more static religion. The number of people being evangelized had been increasing until that time, but once the Christian faith became, in effect, the religion of the establishment in Central and Western Europe, the number of unreached likely began to increase until the time of the modern Protestant missions movement initiated by William Carey in the 1790s.[40] There were exceptions, of course, such as the Coptic Church's bringing the gospel to Africa during times of persecution, but the exception proves the rule.

During the sixteenth-century Counter-Reformation, the Catholic Church assigned the mission to elite orders of professional missionaries in religious orders, such as the Jesuits, to bring the Catholic faith to new territories. While the Catholic branch of the Church established structures for carrying out the Great Commission long before the Reformed branch, the problem inherent in their approach was that it tended to exclude ordinary believers from participating in the mission.

The use of religious orders for Great Commission work established a paradigm that generally excluded the participation of local congregations.[41] While establishing missional structures to advance the faith was a very positive step, it served to establish the special call to missions at the expense of the general call.

After the Reformation, the Protestant Church, except during renewal movements, did little in carrying out the Great Commission for all nations, mainly because most in the Protestant church mistakenly believed the Apostles had already fulfilled Christ's Commission.[42] The error was not corrected until Carey's *Enquiry* was published in 1792. He pointed out that since the promise of Christ's presence in Matthew 28:18–20 was "to the end of the age," the mandate to which it was attached must likewise be binding throughout the Church Age until the gospel was preached to all nations.[43] After the publication of the *Enquiry*, the Protestant Church began to create structures in the form of mission societies to advance the Christian faith to new areas. However, for the most part, it also recovered only one of the two paradigms seen in Acts, the special call but not the general call to missions.

Before leaving the topic of the Church's failure in relation to bringing the gospel to all nations in spite of having two thousand years to do so, it's helpful to consider how the Lord deals with our sin and failure.

> He does not deal with us according to our sins,
>   nor repay us according to our iniquities.
> For as high as the heavens are above the earth,
>   so great is his steadfast love toward those who fear him. (Psalm 103:10–11)

Though we have passed from death to life, we are not instantly or completely sanctified in this life. For this reason, the Father deals with us patiently and graciously. Think about how Jesus dealt with Peter and his initial failure to stay with Jesus through his great trial. Not really knowing his own heart, Peter had boasted, "Even if all fall away on account of you, I never will" (Matthew 26:33). But when the test came, Peter fled in fear only to end up weeping bitterly. God used the episode to wean him off his self-confidence and to position him to receive the baptism of the Holy Spirit.

Jesus didn't abandon Peter when he failed. He understood him perfectly, engineered his failure for the greater good, restored him gently in due time, and reinstated him in his place of leadership in the Church. In the power of the Holy Spirit, Peter would go on to be used by God to advance the Kingdom in great and mighty ways. The Lord deals with his Church today in the same way, gently leading and not condemning, sovereignly working all for good. As Tim Keller often said, "We are more sinful and flawed in ourselves than we ever dared believe, yet at the very same time, we are more loved and accepted in Jesus Christ than we ever dared hope."

In the next section, we'll look at the solution to this great problem of the rising number of unreached. Not surprisingly, the solution is found not in ourselves but in Christ. In Jesus' Last Discourse, he plainly tells us how to effectively carry out his final command.

Questions for Reflection and Discussion

1. Why were the disciples slow to see that the Good News was for the Gentiles as well as the Jewish people?

2. What significant role did the ordinary Christians of the early church play in starting the first church beyond Judea and Samaria?

3. What can modern Christians learn from these early believers?

PART TWO

THE SOLUTION: CHRIST'S VISION FOR HIS MISSION

> Nothing is more powerful than an idea whose time has come.
> —Victor Hugo

Victor Hugo said the most powerful thing on earth is an idea whose time has come, but in reality, there is something even more powerful: a vision from God whose time has come. Jesus' vision for his mission is such a vision. His vision and plan provide the solution to the problem of the growing number of unreached in two ways. First, since he prays that we might be one so the world will know the Father has sent him, it calls us to put aside secondary differences and come together as one for the sake of carrying out the Great Commission.

Second, his vision implies that every Christian is a missionary. Of course, most Christians are not called to be missionaries in the technical sense of being sent out to do cross-cultural church planting. This is a special call from God, and such a call is indispensable.

But there is a second kind of call to the mission of God: the general call.

> And he gave the apostles, the prophets, the evangelists, the shepherds and teachers, to equip the saints for the work of ministry . . . (Ephesians 4:11–12)

Those who are given the special call to be apostles and evangelists are called not just to do the work of missions and evangelism, but also to equip God's people for "the work of ministry." The Reformation idea of the "priesthood of the believer" is thoroughly biblical and provides part of the paradigm for the needed "game changer" in world missions. It implies every believer is a "priest" or minister.

In these two ways, Jesus addresses the need for cooperation and sufficient manpower to bring the gospel to all nations.

Chapter 4

What the Bible is Really All About

> "Not called!" did you say? "Not heard the call,"
> I think you should say. Put your ear down to the
> Bible, and hear Him bid you go and pull sinners
> out of the fire of sin. Put your ear down to the
> burdened, agonized heart of humanity,
> and listen to its pitiful wail for help.
> —William Booth

When I first came to faith, I knew nothing about the Bible. Providentially, I started attending Fourth Presbyterian Church in Bethesda, Maryland. The senior pastor was Dr. Richard C. Halverson, one of the great Christian leaders of the past generation.

As a young man, I started to attend because Fourth had a large, excellent Christian singles ministry in the 1970s. But once I started worshipping there, I was drawn by Dr. Halverson's powerful preaching. He was one of the last of the old-style preachers. He preached the gospel with great authority and in the power of the Holy Spirit rather than in the more conversational style more popular today.

I distinctly remember the first sermon I heard there, which was about faith in Christ as the positive alternative to "secular humanism." Halverson described humanism as fallen man putting faith in fallen man's ability to perfect himself. As a former believer in humanistic psychology, I saw the futility of that in comparison to the sure hope to be found in Jesus Christ. I had attended the National Science Foundation Behavioral Science Institute one summer as a high school student, majored in psychology, and had been accepted into a top PhD program. But with all my knowledge of psychology, I couldn't even solve my own problems.

But another of his sermons on the fulness of the Holy Spirit, caused me to question one of his points. Even though I was a new believer, I had experienced the Baptism of the Holy Spirit through attending a Charismatic Episcopal church. Dr. Halverson preached a sermon that suggested the idea that being filled with the Spirit was a one-time event.

Since I had recently been filled with the Spirit and since I had read in the Book of Acts that the Spirit came upon the believers not only at Pentecost, but also in Acts 4:31, 8:17, and 11:15, I wrote a letter to Dr. Halverson questioning the idea that being filled with the Spirit was a one-time event. He invited me to meet with him to discuss the point.

I have to say that he was very gracious with me, since I was very new in the faith and knew and understood very little about the Bible. At the time, I had no idea that he was a respected, nationally known leader of very high stature. He had been serving as chairman of the board of World Vision for some years and would be called in a few years to serve as the chaplain of the US Senate. Had I known these things, I might not have dared to write him, questioning one of his statements. He must have seen I was a young man lacking in humility and in need of discipleship, and he invited me to meet with him for discipleship training shortly thereafter.

Interestingly, many years later I came to discover that he himself had been part of a special visitation of the Holy Spirit at Forest Home retreat center in California in 1947. Noted Bible teacher Henrietta Mears brought together four young men for prayer before this significant visitation of the Spirit. She had recently returned from Europe, where she saw the devastation and hopelessness after World War II, to address a large conference of Bible teachers and pastors. Her trusted companion Ethel Baldwin wrote:

> As she . . . stepped on the boat to return to America, Miss Mears felt a growing awareness of God's leading . . . felt she was being moved forward by an unseen hand.
>
> As the hundreds of Sunday School workers, pastors, and young seminarians listened, she spelled out all she had seen abroad. . . . "There is no mystery as to what has happened to Germany. It can all be traced step by step. And the same is happening in America today. There must be a Christian answer to the growing menace of communism. . . . God has an answer. Jesus said we must make disciples of all men. We are to take his gospel to the ends of the earth. We must become evangelists even though evangelism is not recognized in our day as valid program. . . . God is looking for men and women of total commitment. . . . We must become expendables for Christ."

She spoke of the need for prayer, revival, and the Word. Four men in particular, along with a number of others, responded to the call and gathered together for prayer. Richard Halverson, the associate pastor of First Presbyterian Church in Hollywood; Bill Bright, a recent convert; Louis Evans, the pastor's son; and John Franck, one of Mears's assistants. As they knelt, they were overcome by the sense of their own inadequacy and powerlessness. They confessed their sins and earnestly sought the Lord. Then the fire from heaven fell, bestowing on them vision and power for evangelism.[44]

Halverson later commented, "Although we were not soliciting any special work of the Spirit that evening, He seemed to meet us in special power, and the meeting turned into an unusual period of blessing and spiritual planning." Bright said, "We were overwhelmed by the presence of God . . . and I didn't know what to do. I just got on my knees and began to praise the Lord." Evans wondered, "What could happen if we, the [members of the] College Department, really gave our lives to Christ?"[45]

Richard Halverson would go on to lead Fourth Presbyterian Church in Washington, DC, to disciple many future Christian leaders, author numerous books, serve as chairman of World Vision, and as chaplain of the Senate. Bill Bright would found Cru, one of the largest mission organizations. Louis Evans would serve as pastor of National Presbyterian Church in Washington, DC. Others who were touched by this move of God in Hollywood at that time included Billy Graham and Jim Rayburn, the founder of Young Life. Also present at Forest Home was J. Edwin Orr, an avid follower of Christ and student of revival. He would go on to serve as a professor of world missions at Fuller Seminary and write prolifically on the history of spiritual awakenings.

Halverson discipled young men using an outline of the Bible which clearly shows the theme is the mission of God. Even though the Bible was written by some forty different authors over a period of fifteen hundred years, it all fits together perfectly around this central narrative. The theme might be expressed in this way:

In love, God redeems a people for himself from every tribe, nation, and tongue in, through, and for Jesus Christ; then God the Holy Spirit applies that redemption as the Church carries out the Great Commission.

The outline of the Bible, below, shows how all the parts fit together around this theme of redemption:

1. The Occasion for Redemption: Genesis 1–11

2. The Preparation for Redemption: Genesis 12–Malachi

3. The Manifestation of Redemption: The Four Gospels

4. The Propagation of Redemption: Acts

5. The Interpretation of Redemption: The Epistles

6. The Consummation of Redemption: The Revelation

I began to learn the redemptive mission of God is the "scarlet thread of redemption," which runs throughout the Bible from cover to cover. God's great redemptive mission is not just mentioned in the Bible: it's the central narrative. A more detailed, simplified version of this outline can be found in Appendix A. Memorizing the six main categories is a helpful way of grasping the "grand narrative."

Questions for Reflection and Discussion

1. Is God's great redemptive mission the central theme of the Bible? Why or why not?

2. If the redemptive mission of God is the "grand narrative" of the Bible, how does that affect your understanding of the Christian faith?

Chapter 5

Is the Great Commission Only for Professional Missionaries?

> The Great Commission will not be fulfilled by somebody trying to reach everybody, but by everybody trying to reach somebody.
> —John Flack

Richard and Michelle's daughter Julie asked her folks if she could go on a short-term mission to the Arab Festival in Dearborn, Michigan, during her summer break. Money was tight for the family, and her dad asked he why she needed to go. Julie said most of these Arab friends had no chance to hear the gospel, and her youth group would hand out tracts and engage people in conversations about Jesus and the gospel.

Richard answered, "Isn't that what the missionaries and ministers are supposed to do?"

Julie, who had been reading a book by John Piper, quoted Piper in her reply: "Go, send, or disobey."

Before we consider the question of who is responsible for carrying out the Great Commission, it's helpful to look at the five versions Jesus gave of his commission.

The most detailed version is in Matthew's gospel:

> And Jesus came and said to them, "All authority in heaven and on earth has been given to me. Go therefore and make disciples of all nations, baptizing them in the name of the Father and of the Son and of the Holy Spirit, teaching them to observe all that I have commanded you. And behold, I am with you always, to the end of the age." (Matthew 28:18–20)

Matthew emphasizes taking the initiative, making disciples cross-culturally, and integrating them into the Church. Mark emphasizes world evangelization:

> And he said to them, "Go into all the world and proclaim the gospel to the whole creation. Whoever believes and is baptized will be saved, but whoever does not believe will be condemned." (Mark 16:15–16)

Luke records that the disciples will be witnesses of Christ's death and resurrection once empowered by the Holy Spirit:

> "Thus it is written, that the Christ should suffer and on the third day rise from the dead, and that repentance for the forgiveness of sins should be proclaimed in his name to all nations, beginning from Jerusalem. You are witnesses of these things. And behold, I am sending the promise of my Father upon you. But stay in the city

until you are clothed with power from on high." (Luke 24:46–49)

In John's version, Jesus emphasizes he is sending them with delegated authority to bring the forgiveness of sins:

> Jesus said to them again, "Peace be with you. As the Father has sent me, even so I am sending you." And when he had said this, he breathed on them and said to them, "Receive the Holy Spirit. If you forgive the sins of any, they are forgiven them; if you withhold forgiveness from any, it is withheld." (John 20:21–23)

Finally, in Acts, Jesus foretells their empowerment by the Holy Spirit to be witnesses to the end of the earth:

> "But you will receive power when the Holy Spirit has come upon you, and you will be my witnesses in Jerusalem and in all Judea and Samaria, and to the end of the earth." (Acts 1:8)

Clearly Christ commanded *his disciples* to go and preach the gospel and make disciples among all nations in the power of the Holy Spirit, baptizing them into his Church. But is the Great Commission binding only on the original disciples?

As we've seen, after the Reformation many thought so, but God used the modern Protestant missions movement founder, William Carey, to correct this mistake.

Today many Christians assume that the Great Commission only applies to the church leaders—the pastors, evangelists and particularly to the career missionaries. But is this a correct assumption?

Some believe that doing missions is only for those who have been called to go and plant the church cross-culturally. We can't deny that those with this special call are the indispensable tip of the spear. As missions professor David Hesselgrave has written:

> The primary mission of the Church, and therefore, of the churches, is to proclaim the gospel of Christ and gather believers into local churches where they can be built up in the faith and made effective in service, thereby planting new congregations throughout the world.[46]

The essential task of the Christian mission is cross-cultural church planting, and clearly, this is the work for specially gifted and trained leaders. God works especially through leaders, but does that mean, therefore, the Great Commission applies *only* to missionaries and other full-time leaders? **This is the crux of the most consequential issue facing the Church today.** God has used the career missionaries to bring the gospel of his kingdom to the countless millions who have not yet heard. This requires preparation, cost, commitment, and sacrifice on their part.

But we cannot relegate the task to them alone. God has called their family of faith back home to stand with them in faith, solidarity, and support. If you will excuse the war analogy, Jesus' vision implies an effort more like the unified allied victory of World War II than the uncommitted, divided effort in the Vietnam War. The allies won WWII because it was a united, concerted effort, but the Vietnam War was doomed to failure largely because of divisions and lack of support.

Rousing the sleeping giant, i.e., mobilizing the Body of Christ for a concerted effort with "all hands on deck" may well be the game changer that brings the gospel to the ends of the earth. Evangelizing reaches some, bringing linear growth. Making disciples reaches more, producing geometric growth. **But recovering the general call to missions as part of the Christian identity holds the potential of reaching the world, producing unstoppable, exponential growth.**

Perhaps a better way to frame the question is, "Did the Lord entrust his sacred mission to the professional missionaries only, or to the church as a whole?"

Consider the case for believing the Lord intends to work through the Church as a whole, and not through the professional missionaries alone. The following are several convincing biblical and practical reasons for believing he intends to work through the whole Body of Christ.

Image of God Principle

The triune God works in concert for our redemption, working as the divine family. The Father, the Son, and the Holy Spirit work in concert in creation, providence, and redemption. In redemption, the Father loves, plans, and sends; the Son accepts the mission of redeeming the elect from all nations and accomplishes it; he does so in humble dependence on the Father and the Holy Spirit in perfect union and concert with them. Even though our Lord Jesus Christ accomplished redemption, he did not do so autonomously, independently, or in isolation from the other persons of the Godhead. Since the triune God has accomplished our redemption in unison, it is not surprising that the Church as a body, in union with the Trinity, should be instrumental in the task of propagating that redemption. As God is, so we are. And as God works, so we work.

The Church as the Body of Christ

The Apostle Paul reveals the Church is the Body of Christ, and it works only in concert, with each of its parts working in a mutually dependent way. If the eye cannot say to the hand, "I don't need you," then the career missionaries and the congregation back home who sends and supports them need each other.[47]

The Role of Ministers and the Priesthood of Believers

God calls ordained ministers and missionaries not only to do the work of ministry, but also to equip God's people to do so:

> And He Himself gave some to be apostles, some prophets, some evangelists, and some pastors and teachers, for the equipping of the saints for the work of ministry, for the edifying of the body of Christ. (Ephesians 4:11–12, NKJ)

This view of the role of ordained teaching elders is both Reformed and biblical. The Apostle Peter proclaimed that the believer is a member of a "royal priesthood." The Westminster Confession is widely considered to be one of the greatest expressions of the Reformed faith in the English language. The 1903 addition to the Confession affirms the priesthood of the believer, especially in relation to the Great Commission, in this way:

> . . . Christ hath commissioned his church to go into all the world and to make disciples of all nations. All believers are, therefore, under obligation to sustain the ordinances of the Christian religion where they are already established and to contribute by their prayers, gifts, and personal efforts to the extension of the kingdom of Christ throughout the whole earth.

THE EXAMPLE OF THE EARLY CHURCH

We have already seen in Chapter 3 that while the eleven were slow to leave Jerusalem and bring the gospel to the ancient world, ordinary Christians took the lead. Deacons Stephen and Philip were quick to be witnesses in Judea and Samaria, and the ordinary Christians who were scattered first preached the gospel to the Gentiles and planted the Church beyond Judea and Samaria around 40 AD. This was about six years before the Council of Jerusalem finally settled the question of the Gentiles, and Paul's first missionary journey.[48]

Clearly in the early church, ordinary Christians knew that carrying out the Great Commission was part of following Christ. The notion that one could believe in him and follow him but ignore the task he entrusted to them never occurred to them.

In the early church, ordinary Christians, working in partnership with the Eleven and the Apostle Paul, played significant and, at times, even leading roles in advancing the gospel among the unreached.

THE EXAMPLE OF THE AWAKENED CHURCH

In his landmark book outlining the essential primary and secondary elements of revival in church history, church historian Richard Lovelace outlines five secondary elements, which are the fruit of moves of the Holy Spirit. The first of these is an orientation to missions.[49]

Lovelace found that a heart for missions flows from spiritual renewal:

> The secondary conditions of renewal are also closely connected with our union with Christ, and they flow out of the primary elements secured in the atonement. *Orientation toward mission* relates Christ's work to the rest

of the world, and it is essentially involved in knowing and following the Holy Spirit and correctly using our authority against the powers of darkness.[50]

Lovelace documents that whenever the sleeping giant wakes up, there is a renewed interest in the advance of God's kingdom through proclaiming the Good News to those who haven't heard. Two examples illustrate this awakened concern. Consider the example of Jonathan Edwards, who was instrumental in the First Great Awakening. Edwards himself became a missionary to Native Americans at the outpost of Stockbridge, Massachusetts, during the final seven years of his life.[51]

Similarly, when the Holy Spirit visited the Moravian Church led by Count Zinzendorf beginning in 1727, one in four of them became missionaries. Some of them were willing to sell themselves into slavery to save the unreached African slaves in the West Indies.[52] Pastor John Piper tells their story this way:

> After Zinzendorf had finished the university, he took a trip throughout Europe looking at some of the cultural highspots. And something very unexpected happened. In the art museum at Dusseldorf he saw a painting by Domenico Feti entitled *Ecce Homo* ("Behold the Man"). It was a portrait of Christ with the crown of thorns pressed down on his head and blood running down his face.
>
> Beneath the portrait were the words, "I have done this for you; what have you done for me?" All of his life Zinzendorf looked back to that encounter as utterly life-changing. As he stood there, as it were, watching his Savior suffer and bleed, he said to himself, "I have loved him for a long time, but I have never actually done anything for him. From now on I will do whatever he leads me to do."

For the rest of his life the blood of Jesus had a central place in the doctrine and devotion of Zinzendorf and his community at Herrnhut. And the story goes that when the first two young missionaries boarded the ship in Copenhagen to sail for the West Indies, perhaps never to return (twenty out of the first twenty-nine missionaries to St. Thomas and St. Croix died in those first years), they lifted their hands as if in sacred pledge and called out to their friends on shore, "May the Lamb that was slain receive the reward of his suffering!"[53]

THE MAGNITUDE OF THE TASK

There is a very practical reason to mobilize the church for world evangelization: the sheer magnitude of the task. According to the Joshua Project, there are still some 3.4 billion unreached peoples in some 7,250 people groups[54]. However, there are only approximately 430,000 career missionaries worldwide, of whom only about 3.3% are engaged in evangelism among unreached peoples.

This means that the ratio of professional missionaries to unreached people is about 1 missionary for every 7,900 unreached. However, the ratio of Christians to unreached peoples is about 1 Christian for every 1.4 unreached persons. ***Mobilizing God's people brings the mission task within reach, even if only a fraction of Christians realize God's mission is for them.***

COMPLETE UNITY OF THE BODY ESSENTIAL FOR WORLD EVANGELIZATION

The most potent argument for the universal application of the Great Commission comes from the words of the Lord Jesus himself. He prayed that the Church might be one so that the world would know that the Father had sent him (John 17:20–23). Our Lord's Prayer reveals that "complete unity" (17:23, NIV) of the Body of Christ is essential for world evangelization. Since every Christian is essential for the complete unity of the church, it follows that every Christian is essential for world evangelization.

This prayer is part of a longer passage in the gospel of John known as The Last Discourse (John 13–17). Here Jesus reveals his vision and plan for the fulfillment of his Great Commission. In the next chapter, we will look more closely at that great discourse and the vision Jesus reveals for fulfilling his mission. Jesus' vision and the logic inherent in his High Priestly prayer effectively settle the matter.

Case Study: Jeremiah, African Farmer and Tentmaker

Jeremiah is a young man from West Africa who serves the Lord as a self-supporting pastor, church planter, and translator. He was once an idol worshipper but came to faith through the work of missionaries who came to his village. He now overflows with joy as he serves the Lord with his whole heart.

How did you come to faith?

It was in 1993 when the missionaries came from the US. And they sent missionaries to our village to preach the gospel. Now, first of all, I just want to say that I was an animist because I was in a family where we just worshipped idols.

And now when they came, they showed a movie about Jesus Christ. We were able to hear Jesus Christ himself speak in our mother tongue, Gourma. And when I was watching, I was very interested to hear the characters in the film, especially Jesus Christ, speaking in our mother tongue.

So if I want to summarize, being a Christian changed my life a lot because I could see the difference between one who worships idols and a Christian. And until now I have been very happy because when I was not a Christian, I was not having any joy. But now I have the peace that Jesus Christ has given me. No matter the circumstances, no matter the problems of life, all the time I'm still in peace. I'm still in joy, so I'm very happy to share my story with you, to show how I met Jesus Christ.

How did you take up your vocation?

I'm very happy being a pastor, the vocation I'm called to. I will say that I'm just full of joy, 100%. I'm embracing it. Because I could not, I did not deserve it.

Now I put all my efforts, all my power into it, in order to work for God. So, that means being a pastor, and praying for people, and translating the Bible, and especially planting churches.

It's not easy, I know. I took my courage in two hands. And I said, as I was saying to my wife, no matter the circumstances, I'll give all my last breath for God. Because he has done many things for me, things that I did not deserve. It is by grace that he gave them to me. So, I just ask myself, what can I give in return to Christ? Now I just want to give all my body, all my mind, all my time with pleasure, in order to serve him.

When I became a pastor in 2018, they sent me to a village. And when I went there, the pastor was not earning anything. There was a small stipend for people planting churches, about $10.

But after three years, they paid me about $30. But they transferred me there because I was called to go and translate the Bible. And when I came to the church I am pastoring, let me tell you that there was nothing in the way of support.

But then I started doing translation. I am not yet an official translator, but they are giving us something in the way of payments. But we are not yet official translators. In July we will go to the city to make a final text. That final text will determine who will be chosen to translate the Bible. I have confidence in Jesus that they will select me by grace.

I am very passionate in working because I like farming and taking care of animals. And that will give me money in order to support my myself and my family. I have a wife and three children, with another on the way. We have a boy and a girl. I encountered a boy there who was very sick. And I prayed for him, and he was healed. We call him Isaiah. His parents transferred him to me, and now we are taking care of him.

What motivates you in the mission?

What motivates me to do my work? I can say that it is what Jesus Christ has done for me, the great things that our Lord Jesus Christ has done for me. That is the key motivation for me, for my work.

And I'm seeing it like an obligation, even moral obligation, for me to work. I want to work for the Lord, to give all my time to the Lord, because our lives depend on him. It is by grace that we are living. And if it is by grace that I'm living, why can't I pay back to the Lord? I cannot. So, if I were to work, for example, for money or people or anything else, I should be discouraged one day. Because if it is people who motivate me, they may disappoint. And if it is money that motivates me, what will happen in the day the money stops? In that day, what can I do? It means I will forsake the work of God.

It is what God or Jesus Christ has done on the cross for me. And I see my life is grace. Everything that I have is for him, even my personal life. It's for him. I am only the steward of all I have, but God is the owner.

What advice would you give to others?

I will say put your total confidence in the Lord. Put your total confidence in God because it is only God who will help us. Only he can sustain you and qualify you. I also say that if you want to serve the Lord, don't be counting on people. Don't be counting on money. Don't be counting on your competencies. Be counting on the Lord only.

And don't be waiting for something like a reward before you can work in the service of the Lord. Just look at Jesus Christ on the cross, at what Jesus Christ has done for you on the cross. And if you see what Jesus Christ has done on the cross for you, then you will serve.

Only Jesus Christ. I would tell everybody, every servant of God, that the real supporter in the ministry of the Lord is the Lord himself.

And the real person who is going to encourage us is not a human being. It is the Lord himself.

And I also see people like Paul, who were living by faith. I can see many people of God living by faith, and we also have to. But if I want to give any advice, I will tell my friends, my coworkers, "Let us live by faith, counting only on God. And it shall be an open door to every blessing. The closed shall be open to us."

I want to tell them that doing that work, doing things that way, is not easy. There will come a time that you will say, "It is better for me to stop being a servant of God." But if you persevere and stand fast in all things, in the end, the Lord will bless you.

Questions for Reflection and Discussion

1. What is the role of the career missionary in relation to the Great Commission?

2. What is the role of ordinary believers in relation to Christ's Commission?

3. What are the similarities and differences between the roles?

4. What are examples of each type of role in the New Testament?

Chapter 6

Jesus' Vision for the Mission: The Last Discourse—A Blueprint for the Last Command

> The missionary enterprise is no human conception
> or undertaking, no modern scheme or invention . . .
> It did not originate in the brain or heart of any man,
> not even William Carey, or the Apostle Paul. Its
> source was in the heart of God Himself. And Jesus
> Christ, God's great Missionary to a lost world, was
> the supreme revelation of His heart and
> expression of His love.
> —Robert Hall Glover, missionary to China

What do you think is the most consequential Bible passage in relation to the mission of the Church, after the Great Commission?

Some scholars consider the Last Discourse to be the most consequential passage in the most important book of the Bible, at least in relation to the continuation of the mission of God. Why? For one thing, it presents Jesus' longest discourse in the Bible, longer even than the Sermon on the Mount. For another, John was the disciple closest to Jesus, and so held a most privileged position. He alone records the intimate communication of the Son with his Father before his death in the High Priestly Prayer (John 17:1–26). As we approach to listen in, we need to take off our shoes and draw near with fear and trembling because we are entering into the Holy of Holies to hear an extended, intimate interchange between the members of the Holy Trinity.

All scripture is inspired by God, but not all scripture is equally weighty. The scriptures employ various methods to emphasize certain truths over others, such as repetition, as seen in the Gospels themselves and in the case of the Great Commission. We expect the last words of any great man to hold special significance; how much more those of the very Son of God.

Another means the Bible uses to emphasize certain passages is by means of its literary genre. **The Last Discourse is a *testament*.** The testament is a common ancient literary genre. In the ancient world, a great man would gather his children or his followers to tell them how he wanted his affairs handled after his death. **It has the same force as a Last Will and Testament in the modern world, the legally binding directives for those left behind.** No one would even consider ignoring the mandates of a lawfully executed last will.

On the eve of his death, having gathered his children or followers together, he entrusts to them the things of their covenant-making, covenant-keeping God. Typically, the testament would include a recounting God's promises and faithfulness to his people, warnings against covenant unfaithfulness, and a prophetic pronouncement of blessings. It signifies passing the torch from the patriarch to the next generation of God's people. Examples include the farewell and blessing of Jacob to his children (Genesis 47:29–49:33), Joshua's farewell to Israel (Joshua 23–24), and David's farewell speech (1 Chronicles 28–29).[55]

The purpose of these Old Covenant testaments is for the departing leader of God's covenant people to pass the baton of leadership to a new generation of leaders of God's people. The generations would come and go, but the sacred covenant relationship between God and his people continued over time.

The context is the unfolding narrative of God's redemptive mission for Israel, and through Israel to every nation under heaven. These events are not merely a reading of the will for a personal estate to convey a few bits of property and perhaps some minor title. These patriarchs are conscious that Almighty God has called them out of worshipping worthless idols into a unique covenant relationship with himself. They recall God's calling of Abram and his covenantal promises.

God showed Abram all the stars in the heavens and promised him "so shall your offspring be" (Gen. 15:5). He further promised an everlasting covenant with him and his offspring, and that all the nations of the earth would be blessed through him (Genesis 17:1-8, 22:17–18).

The covenant promises to Abraham were solemn reminders that the children of Israel were heirs of the eternal promises of Almighty God and that they had the privilege of being part of the great story, the mission of God. They knew that God had called them and that somehow, in God's economy, they had the unique privilege of being instrumental in bringing the blessings of Almighty God to all the other nations of the earth.

God uses these occasions to reveal his sovereign will in advancing his purposes. In the case of David, even though David wanted to build a temple for God, the Lord revealed he had in fact chosen Solomon for that privilege. In the case of Jacob and Esau, God chose Jacob but not Esau, even though Esau was the elder brother (Genesis 27:1–40, Romans 9:12).

Just before the Last Discourse, Jesus washes the disciples' feet. At the time, the disciples would not understand what Jesus was doing (13:7). We are witnessing the perfect humility of God the Son, come into the world to cleanse a people for himself. After the meal, the cleansing is complete with the departure of Judas Iscariot (John 13:30).

God will call upon these men to lay down their lives for the sake of Christ and the gospel. So Jesus uses the occasion to prepare them for the sacred mission that will cost them everything. He tells them plainly that they will have tribulation because the world will hate them just as it hated him (John 15:18, 16:33) But they are to take heart because he has overcome the world and is going to take them to the place he has prepared for them in heaven (John 14:2–3, 16:33).

In his Last Discourse, Jesus gives his Church a command, a promise, a provision, and a prayer. The promise of greater works and the prayer "that the world will know" indicate that the Last Discourse is all about the continuation of the mission of God. Jesus guarantees the ultimate success of the Church's mission with his High Priestly prayer.

THE COMMAND

First, Jesus gives his disciples a new commandment: to love one another as he has loved them (John 13:34). But wasn't the command—to love—an old commandment? True, the command to love was not new, but loving as Jesus loved was new. No one had ever seen perfect, self-sacrificing, extravagant love incarnate. No one had ever before seen the full revelation of God's love for his people. The bar had been raised.

He sums up their new way of life in the Kingdom of God: Love one another. How has he loved them? Freely, fully, and forever. He loves them freely because his love is a gracious gift. They have done nothing to deserve it and can do nothing to lose it. He loves fully because he holds nothing back, even his own blood! He loves them forever because he has entered into a new, eternal covenant with them. A covenant is, by nature, an unbreakable agreement.

The love command is foundational to all that follows. And he attaches the most amazing promise, provision, and prayer to ensure their success in continuing to carry on the mission of God by bringing the gospel to the nations.

The Promise

Second, Jesus goes on to make a series of astounding promises to the disciples if they will obey this New Commandment. First, they will do the works Jesus did, and amazingly, even greater works (14:12), and whatever they ask in prayer will be granted (14:13–14). Furthermore, the Father, the Son, and the Holy Spirit will come and dwell in them if they love him and keep his commandments (John 14:16–22). The promised greater works come mainly in relation to world evangelization. Jesus reached a relatively small number of people from one ethnic group in his earthly ministry in Judea; he will now reach people of all nations through the work of his global Church. The works will be greater because it will be God the Holy Spirit doing the work through a vast worldwide community of faith over time, and no longer just through a single man, in one particular place, during a brief three-year period. In this way, they will be like a branch "that bears much fruit" (15:5).

As astounding as the promise of doing greater works than Jesus did and having a "blank check" for answered prayers, there is an even more wonderful promise here for those who respond to Christ's extravagant love with extravagant love expressed in obedience. The Father will love them. The Savior will love them and manifest himself to them. The triune God will make his home with them (John 14:21, 23). How can we understand the promise of love here? Doesn't the Father and the Son already love the believer?

It is one thing to be loved but another to enter into the fulness of an awakened love relationship. Like the bride in the Song of Solomon:

> My beloved speaks and says to me:
>
> "Arise, my love, my beautiful one,
>   and come away,
>
> for behold, the winter is past . . ."
> (Song of Solomon 2:8-11)

Jonathan Edwards described entering into the love of God in this way:

> Sometimes, only mentioning a single word caused my heart to burn within me; or only seeing the name of Christ, or the name of some attribute of God. And God has appeared glorious to me, on account of the Trinity. It has made me have exalting thoughts of God, that he subsists in three persons; Father, Son and Holy Ghost . . .
>
> Once, as I rode out into the woods for my health, in 1737, having alighted from my horse in a retired place, as my manner commonly has been, to walk for divine contemplation and prayer, I had a view that for me was extraordinary, of the glory of the Son of God, as Mediator between God and man, and his wonderful, great, full, pure and sweet grace and love, and meek and gentle condescension. This grace that appeared so calm and sweet, appeared also great above the heavens. The person of Christ appeared ineffably excellent with an excellency great enough to swallow up all thought and conception . . . which continued as near as I can judge, about an hour; which kept me the greater part of the time in a flood of tears, and weeping aloud. I felt an ardency of soul to be, what I know not otherwise how to express, emptied and annihilated; to lie in the dust, and to be full of Christ alone; to love him with a holy and pure love . . . [56]

Think about the great people you might want to become friends with but never can. But here in his Last Discourse,

Jesus himself and God the Father give his followers—and us—their intimate friendship and manifest presence (John 14:21, 15:15). This is the amazing promise we have in the gospel!

THE PROVISION

Third, Jesus gives his glory to his Church that we might be his witnesses:

> I do not ask for these only, but also for those who will believe in me through their word, that they may all be one, just as you, Father, are in me, and I in you, that they also may be in us, so that the world may believe that you have sent me. *The glory that you have given me I have given to them* . . . (John 17:21–23)

This prayer is not only for the disciples but, says Jesus, "for those who will believe in me through their word." He prays for you and me, and for all who will believe the testimony of those eye-witnesses down through history.

How are we to understand Christ giving us his glory, given that Isaiah reveals God will not give his glory to another? "I am the Lord; that is my name; my glory I give to no other" (Isaiah 42:8). D.A. Carson writes, "Glory commonly refers to the manifestation of God's character or person in a revelatory context."[57] The glory Jesus is talking about here cannot, therefore, refer to the incommunicable glory of God. By definition, this glory belongs to God alone.

Instead, Jesus is speaking of a glory that is communicable, since the Father gave it to him and he now shares it with his people. He is speaking of the moral perfection of the new humanity now revealed in the glory of the new Adam, the Lord Jesus Christ. The Second Adam confers on his people the glory of the image of God, untainted by the sin of the First Adam. In this way, he blesses us "with every spiritual blessing" (Ephesians 1:3). "For our sake he made him to be sin who knew no sin, so that we might become the righteousness of God" (2 Cor. 5:21).

THE PRAYER

Finally, Jesus offers a prayer. He prays that we "may all be one." He asks for a unity just like the unity he enjoys with his Father. This is not merely an organizational unity, such as we find when companies merge under a single board. Such unity, if any unity at all, is far short of the kind of unity Jesus is talking about. Merely uniting as an interdenominational or ecumenical council alone is not enough—not that there is anything wrong with such bodies. Thank God for them. Jesus speaks of something greater!

That greater unity is not mystical unity, which is invisible and often affirmed in theory only, without the union of covenant love enjoyed between the persons of the Holy Trinity.

Rather this kind of unity is born of living out the new commandment to love as he loves us. It is a unity experienced by Christians when they put aside secondary differences of culture and human tradition, and yes, even differences in positions on non-essential theology and practice, for the sake of realizing the new commandment and carrying out the Great Commission together.

It is a unity missionaries in a hostile field sometimes catch a glimpse of as they put aside their secondary differences for the sake of Christ and to advance his Kingdom. It is a union formed out of shared, committed love for Christ and maintained by a shared, committed love for one another. All of the branches of the Church in the Middle East, joining together to present the message of God's love through SAT-7, is an example.

Jesus prays that we might be one just as he is one with the Father and the Spirit:

> That they may all be one, just as you, Father, are in me, and I in you, that they also may be in us . . . (17:21)

He is asking not only that we may be one, but that we might be one with him and with the Father and the Holy Spirit. Here is the uniqueness of the unity he is envisioning. It is a unity born of our union with the living God. The Holy Spirit is poured out not only to empower for the work, but also to manifest the glory of God in the Church.

Notice the inherent logic of the prayer: Jesus asks the Father for A so that B will happen. He asks that we might be one, in order that the world will know that the Father has sent him. **This means that the unity of the Church is the necessary condition for world evangelization.**

The 1999 *Joint Declaration on Justification* was a helpful step in the direction of unity. In this, the Catholic Church joined the Lutheran Federation in declaring we are saved by grace alone through faith. Methodist, Reformed, Anglican, and other branches of the Church have since adopted this declaration.[58]

This agreement about the nature of the gospel of grace helps to set the stage for a united witness for world evangelization which has not been possible for 500 years. German theologian Martin Luther had not intended to divide the Church when he published his Ninety-Five Theses in 1517. But the new wine of the emerging Reformed Church was not compatible with the old wineskin of Western Church of the Late Middle Ages. These two branches of the Church are agreed, again, that we are saved by grace alone. Agreeing on the essential message is a necessary, if not sufficient, step in the unity Christ envisions and prayed for. To be sure, this declaration does not necessarily mean the Catholic and Protestant branches are now in perfect alignment on the question of justification by faith through grace. However, it does at least mean that there are some in the Catholic branch of the Church who understand that salvation is a gracious gift, as there are in other branches of the Church, and who can, therefore, join together in coalitions of the willing to bring the gospel to the unreached.[59]

Returning to the original question of whether God intends to fulfill the Great Commission through professional missionaries alone or through the Body of Christ, it is clear from Jesus' High Priestly prayer that he intends to use the Body of Christ. He will work through the missionaries, but every Christian in every branch of the Church also has the joy and responsibility of being part of this greatest of all enterprises. God calls every branch of the Church to his mission. Again, without each member, how could there be "complete unity" (John 17:23)?

Christ intends to bring the gospel to the nations through his united Body, and each member is indispensable to the perfect unity he calls us to. Individual commitments to the Lord and his mission are made and sustained only in fellowship with others who are called and covenantally bound together to advance God's kingdom. Therefore, every

Christian is essential for the completion of the mission of God, and so every Christian is a missionary, at least in the sense of having the general call to be part of God's mission.

There are a thousand good things Christians can devote themselves to. But should we not devote ourselves first and foremost to what Christ commanded us to do in the manner he envisions? To do otherwise is to make ourselves wiser than God.

Progress often occurs in the Church through the process of recovery, just as progress in the world often happens through discovery. Just as the gospel was recovered through the Protestant Reformation, the Mission of the Church was recovered for Protestants through the modern Protestant Missions Movement. In a similar way, Jesus' vision for carrying on his mission can be recovered as we grasp the sometimes-overlooked missional implications of Jesus' Last Discourse. The Transformational Events in Church History diagram below illustrates these events on a timeline.

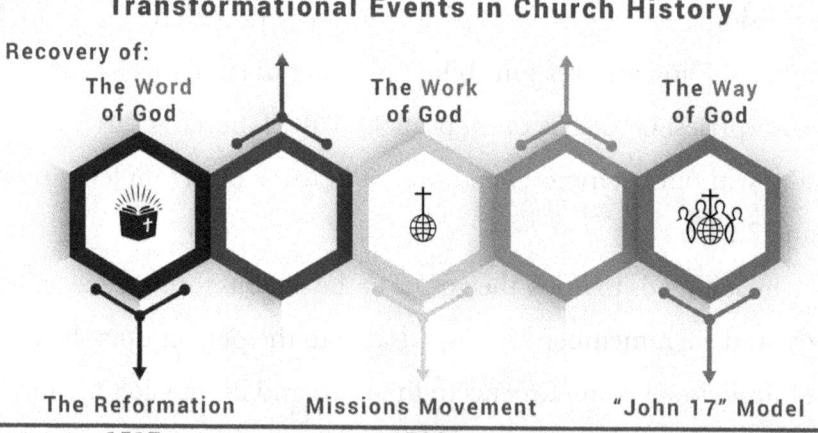

APPLICATION: THE JOHN 17 CORE PRINCIPLES

The John 17 way of doing missions (John 13–17) incorporates the following core principles:

GOD'S MISSION

The central theme of the Bible is God's great redemptive mission in the world. The mission goes far beyond what many conceive of as "missions." To think that missions is based on a few proof texts is to risk missing the point. The Bible is the story of how our holy, loving God redeems people of all nations for his glory in Christ—the mission of God. The Old Testament is largely the preparation for redemption, the gospels record its accomplishment, and the balance of the New Testament records the beginning of its spread, its explanation, and consummation. Having sovereignly and graciously accomplished our redemption through Christ's Great Commission and the power of the Holy Spirit, he graciously grants the Church the honor of serving as the primary instrument for applying this great redemption.

EVERY CHRISTIAN IS A MISSIONARY

Missions is not an optional add-on for the few career missionaries and enthusiasts, but rather an essential for everyone who is serious about following Jesus Christ. The term "evangelical Christian" is therefore redundant. Jesus said, "Follow Me, and I will make you fishers of men." He called the twelve into the mission of God as well as into the life of God. To follow him means having the joy and privilege of being part of what God is doing in the Church age—bringing the gospel to the nations, according to our call and gifting, whether directly or indirectly. As Ford Maddox aptly said, "The first Reformation gave the Word of God to the people of God; we need a second Reformation to give the work of God to the people of God."

The Mission is best accomplished through the Body of Christ

It is clear from Jesus' High Priestly Prayer to the Father recorded in John 17 that he envisions the Body of Christ as the vehicle through which he will bring the gospel to all nations. While God can and does use isolated individuals and groups to accomplish his purposes, his design is that the Holy Spirit apply Christ's great redemption through the Body of Christ as she carries out the Great Commission. The outpouring of the Holy Spirit at Pentecost marked Jesus Christ's passing of the baton to the Church that she might become the primary agency through which God brings his redemption to a broken, ruined world.

Support Strategic Obedience to the Great Commission

With all the authority of heaven and earth, Jesus Christ commands his Church to plant the Church among all ethnic groups. This implies reaching the unreached must be a priority. Furthermore, the magnitude of the task implies that we must strategically use limited human resources to support the extraordinary redemptive works of God as well as his ordinary works. Specifically, we must pray for, foster, participate in, and support moves of the Holy Spirit and church planting movements among the unreached, as well as ordinary evangelism, discipleship, and church planting. The strategic goal is to make receiving the only way of salvation an actual option for individuals in every ethnic group, and not merely a possible option. Therefore, the strategic objective in evangelism is not merely to win converts; it is not merely to make disciples; nor is it just to plant churches. We need to make disciples who make disciples and plant churches that plant churches. The Church is not a static human institution; it is a dynamic, rapidly spreading fire that comes from God.

These principles can easily be remembered using the acronym "GEMS."

Questions for Reflection and Discussion

1. What is a testament in the Bible?

2. Why did John frame Jesus' final discourse as a testament?

3. What are some indications that Jesus' Last Discourse was a vision statement for how his Church is to carry out his mission?

PART THREE

IMPLICATIONS

Chapter 7

Working Together as the Body of Christ

> The whole church, with every believer, is called to God's mission. The historical development of Christian mission, especially in recent centuries, made the Christian faith a truly global religion. At the same time, a monumental task is before us to mobilize the whole church and every Christian for mission. And we live in a time when a radical rethinking of mission is called for and feasible. This will require the whole church to come together, both global and interdenominational, and both mission thinkers and practitioners.
> —Wonsuk Ma

In the fall of 1978, Lynn Bolte and Harrett Whitesides, two students at Gordon-Conwell Seminary, approached missions professor Christy Wilson and told him they felt called to go and work with Nobel Prize winner Mother Theresa of Calcutta. Both were registered nurses. Dr. Wilson suggested they mainly make it a ministry of prayer as they would have little opportunity to use their nursing.

As they were working with Mother Theresa at the Home for the Sick and Dying, a wealthy Hindu woman came to see the work. The women wrote down her name and prayed for her. A few days later, as they walked across Calcutta, a city of some eleven million, to visit some children in an orphanage, they became extremely thirsty. They asked where they could find some tea, as drinking the water there can be dangerous.

A lady said, "Wait right here." She went into a nearby house and then beckoned them inside. Lynn and Harriett entered the beautiful home and sat down. Who should walk into the room but the same wealthy woman they had been praying for! They shared the gospel with her.

When the Indian nuns of Mother Theresa's Sisters of Charity found out that the women were seminary students, they said, "We want to learn more about the Bible. Could you teach us the Scriptures?"

After they returned and shared their experience, twenty-six students went to Calcutta the next summer. Thus started the seminary's Overseas Mission Practicum. The seminary students shared the Scriptures, and the nuns shared what it means to pour out their lives for the sake of the poor in Christ's name. Working together as the Body, with each contributing their gifts, enabled them to have a powerful witness for Christ.

Clearly, Jesus' vision for his mission, as revealed in his High Priestly prayer, implies that the Church must work together if the nations are to be reached with the gospel. Since Jesus considers unity in the Body a precondition for world evangelization, we must accept the fact.

In 1974, the First International Congress on World Evangelization was significant in modern church history in issuing the *Lausanne Covenant*. This covenant called for a renewed effort to carry out the Great Commission as the united Body of Christ:

> We affirm that Christ sends his redeemed people into the world as the Father sent him, and that this calls for a similar deep and costly penetration of the world. We need to break out of our ecclesiastical ghettos and permeate non-Christian society. In the Church's mission of sacrificial service, evangelism is primary. World evangelization requires the whole Church to take the whole gospel to the whole world. The Church is at the very centre of God's cosmic purpose and is his appointed means of spreading the gospel . . .
>
> We affirm that the Church's visible unity in truth is God's purpose.[60]

At the Second International Congress in 1989, in the *Manila Manifesto*, evangelicals reaffirmed the need for unity and cooperation for evangelizing the world:

> The whole gospel has to be proclaimed by the whole church. All the people of God are called to share in the evangelistic task . . .
>
> We deplore the failures in Christian consistency which we see in both Christians and churches: material greed, professional pride and rivalry, competition in Christian service, jealousy of younger leaders, missionary paternalism, the lack of mutual accountability, the loss of Christian standards of sexuality, and racial, social, and sexual discrimination. . . . We acknowledge our continuing

struggles and failures. But we also determine by God's grace to develop integrity in ourselves and in the church.[61]

This manifesto strikes a note of repentance for things that have hindered a united witness in the past and reaffirms a determination to overcome them with God's help.

There is no need for a new call to unity and repentance from the things that hinder it; the need is for the church to heed the calls already given by Jesus Christ Himself as well as the Evangelical branches of the Church.

Beware of the Leaven of the Pharisees

In Matthew 15, the Pharisees and Scribes confronted Jesus because his disciples did not wash their hands when they ate. Jesus cut through their spiritual blindness as he answered them, "And why do you break the commandment of God for the sake of your tradition?" (Matthew 15:3).

Pharisaism is the rigid adherence to human religious traditions without genuine affection for and devotion to God. Ironically, some who hold a high view of scripture seem blind to this pitfall. One writer calls for Christians to reject both evangelicalism and the ecumenical movement on the grounds they are contrary to fundamentalism. Perhaps it's useful to remember that the Pharisees also zealously believed in inerrancy and refused to compromise on issues of doctrine. But their proud doctrinal purity didn't save them from being enemies of God. Our "isms" can be idols if they, rather than Jesus Christ, determine who we are and what we do.

To be sure, matters of essential truth cannot be compromised in the quest for unity; there is no communion between light and darkness. But the unity that Jesus calls us to does not require any compromise of essential truth; it requires a deeper embrace of and expression of that truth.

My Kingdom is Not of This World

Cal Thomas, once a leading figure in the "Moral Majority" of the 1980s in the US, and Ed Dobson, a former confidant of Jerry Falwell, once thought Ronald Reagan's rise gave conservative Christians their greatest opportunity to win the culture wars in the last generation. In their book *Blinded by the Might*, they wrote, "We were on our way to changing America. We had the power to right every wrong and cure every ill." But they soon came to realize the conservative evangelical political Moral Majority movement did not usher in the kingdom of God on earth. If anything, it might well have helped bring about the opposite. "We think it is time to admit that because we are using the wrong weapons, we are losing the battle."[62]

Perhaps Evangelicals were not merely using the wrong weapons; maybe they were in the wrong war in the first place. These are like weapons of straw against ramparts of iron. Politics has been compared to moving the deck chairs on the Titanic; American politics in the twenty-first century has, at times, seemed more like throwing the deck chairs at one another. A spiritual war cannot be won with political weapons, nor can spiritual and moral problems be solved by political and legal solutions. The enemy is not the other party; it is the Prince of Darkness. God is not saving the world; he is redeeming a people for himself out of this world, which will pass away. More recent political movements have no more power to transform hearts than their predecessors, so we must be clear-eyed and realistic about their limitations.

God calls us to participate in the great cosmic death struggle between good and evil. Jesus Christ has prevailed in the spiritual D-Day through his death and resurrection, and he calls his Church to partner in the mop-up operations with the sword of the Spirit. Our task is to advance his Kingdom, not to advance the agenda of any political party. Jesus said his Kingdom is not of this world. The Christian's call is to evangelism, not political activism.

In Essentials Unity, in Non-Essentials Liberty, and in All Things Charity

There is a way to enjoy unity without compromising essential truth. Professor Mark Ross writes:

> Often attributed to great theologians such as Augustine, the above call to unity and liberty with charity comes from an otherwise undistinguished German Lutheran theologian of the early seventeenth century, Rupertus Meldenius. The phrase occurs in a tract on Christian unity written (circa 1627) during the Thirty Years War (1618–1648), a bloody time in European history in which religious tensions played a significant role. The saying has found great favor among subsequent writers such as Richard Baxter, and has since been adopted as a motto by the Moravian Church of North America and the Evangelical Presbyterian Church. Might it serve us well as a motto for every church and for every denomination today?[63]

Starting in 1994, a remarkable outpouring of the Holy Spirit occurred at the Toronto Airport Christian Fellowship. Speakers such as Terry Virgo preached the gospel in depth, and a sociologist reported that nearly 90% of the attendees loved Christ and their spouses more as a result of their experience of the outpouring. Thousands attended from all over the world.[64]

For a number of years leading up to the outpouring of the Holy Spirit in Toronto in 1994–1995, I met with a group of church leaders every week to pray for revival. They were mostly evangelical pastors, but one of those leaders was the late Peter Hocken, a Catholic theologian and leader of the renewal movement within that branch of the Church. Peter was also the secretary of the Society for Pentecostal Studies.

In February 2013, Peter Hocken and Marty Waldman, a leader in the Messianic Jewish Movement, visited Cardinal Jorge Bergoglio in Buenos Aires, Argentina. They laid hands on him and prayed for his upcoming trip to the conclave in Rome. The humble Cardinal packed a small suitcase for the trip, little realizing what God would call him to. Little did Peter and Marty know that they were blessing the future Pope Francis, with whom they had shared the vision of "Toward Jerusalem Council II," an initiative to promote reconciliation between the historic Churches and the Messianic Jewish believers in Yeshua.[65]

I have already mentioned the *Joint Declaration on Justification* of 1999, which acknowledged that Luther was correct in his understanding that justification is the gracious gift of God. Pope Francis has followed up on this doctrinal agreement with clear gestures of Christian reconciliation, friendship, and brotherhood.

On October 16, 2017, the late Pope Francis celebrated the 500th anniversary of the Reformation with Rev. Derek Browning, Moderator of the General Assembly of the Church of Scotland.

Francis said:

> The past cannot be changed, yet today we at last see one another as God sees us. . . . We are first and foremost his children, reborn in Christ through one baptism, and therefore brothers and sisters. For so long, we regarded one another from afar, all too humanly, harboring suspicion, dwelling on differences and errors, and with hearts intent on recrimination for past wrongs.
>
> Now Catholics and Protestants are pursuing the path of humble charity that leads to overcoming division and healing wounds, working together to serve the poor and promote justice, and are standing together to defend the rights of Christians undergoing persecution.[66]

Such humble acts of reconciliation and unity ought to be recognized and accepted as the work of the Holy Spirit, moving his Church inexorably toward the full answer to the Lord Jesus' High Priestly prayer for Christian unity and world evangelization. Please do not misunderstand me here. I am not advocating for or against any particular denomination or branch of the Church. I am advocating we forsake our tribalism for the sake of Christ. I am advocating the attitudes and actions that are consistent with Christ's High Priestly prayer for Christian unity to advance the cause for which he gave his life. Can we take an attitude toward brothers and sisters in other branches of the Church that is consistent with Christ's commandment to love one another and with his High Priestly Prayer?

Pope Leo likewise similarly grasps the implications of Jesus' vision for his mission. He said, "I still consider myself a missionary. My vocation, like that of every Christian, is to be a missionary, to proclaim the Gospel wherever one is."

QUESTIONS FOR REFLECTION AND DISCUSSION

1. Why is it sometimes so difficult for Christians to work with believers from other Christian traditions?

2. What are some practical ways we can overcome the natural tendency toward "tribalism"?

3. What are some examples of Christians coming together to bring the gospel to those who haven't heard?

CHAPTER 8

THE POWER OF OUR UNITED WITNESS

> But you will receive power when the Holy Spirit has
> come upon you, and you will be my witnesses in
> Jerusalem and in all Judea and Samaria,
> and to the end of the earth.
> (ACTS 1:8)

PAK7 IS A COALITION-BASED media ministry that is seeing the peoples of Pakistan transformed by God's love. How is it able to be fruitful in a hard place? The Body of Christ is working together to demonstrate the gospel she proclaims. The global church is partnering with the national church to make Christ and the gospel known. Many branches of the Church have set aside their secondary differences in culture, language, and tradition to make the main thing the main thing.

Jesus' vision for his mission is that we might be his witnesses in union with God and united with one another. United with Almighty God our Father, we have power. And united with one another, we demonstrate the power of the gospel to transform and reconcile. This is our witness for Christ.

The Power of Our Union with God

Jesus commanded his disciples to wait before they go on to be witnesses. Why? Because the power to witness comes only from the fulness of the Holy Spirit.

The words of Arthur T. Pierson, a Presbyterian minister who sounded the trumpet for the Student Volunteer Movement which began in the 1880s, remain true today:

> Pierson wrote in the Missionary Review that three things were needed to finish the Great Commission and evangelize the world: 1) the whole church needed to be involved; 2) evangelistic zeal was needed in the lives of believers; and 3) a baptism of the power of the Holy Spirit.
> On this last point he wrote, "To do this work in twenty years, we must get more Gospel, more vitality . . . The church has money, brains, organizations, rivers of prayer and oceans of sermons, but she lacks in POWER."[67]

The source of the needed power has not been kept a secret, nor has the means of receiving that power. "Ask and it will be given you" (Matthew 7:7). God does not need to be badgered to give what he has promised, but we must be serious, faithful, fervent, and persistent about asking.

The Power of Our United Witness

Jesus reveals that our united witness is essential for reaching the world with the gospel. Why is that? The fallen world, apart from God's grace, generally operates on the principle of self-interest. This principle is extended from the individual to the group through politics. As a result, various groups are often competing with or even fighting one another.

For this reason, families, tribes, nations, races, religious groups, classes, political parties, and nations are often at odds with one another. As of this writing, there are thirty-two major ongoing conflicts in the world today from Afghanistan to Yemen.[68] The US Congress is so bitterly divided that even approving funds to run the government requires repeated major political maneuvering. Religious conflict is also commonplace, even among Christians.

This is why the 1999 *Joint Declaration* is so significant. After centuries of division and disunity, God has granted a measure of reconciliation to help heal a division that for centuries seemed impossible. By God's grace, Christians are able to rise above the principle of self-interest and operate on the God-given principle of love. "By this all people will know that you are my disciples, if you have love for one another" (John 13:35).

Genuine love that transcends the boundaries of nationality, ethnicity, class, and gender is the hallmark of authentic Christian faith. It testifies that God is love and that he reigns in his people, the Church. The world can neither duplicate nor deny this potent witness of the reality of God's Kingdom. A group which operates on the principle of love rather than on the principle of self-interest will stand out like a light in darkness.

Questions for Reflection and Discussion

1. Why did Jesus pray for unity in his Church so that the world might know the Father sent him?

2. Why do missionaries on the field often find that secondary doctrinal issues and differences in denomination make little difference to them?

3. What differences could the common agreement that salvation is a gift of God's grace make in interdenominational mission efforts?

CHAPTER 9

EVERY CHRISTIAN A MISSIONARY?

> Every Christian here is either
> a missionary or an impostor.
> —CHARLES SPURGEON

SOMETIMES THE MOST UNLIKELY people turn out to be pretty fair evangelists. In May of 1855, an eighteen-year-old boy appeared before the deacons of a church in Boston. Raised in a Unitarian church, he was almost completely ignorant of the gospel. But then, a Sunday School teacher shared the gospel with him and urged him to trust Christ.

One of the deacons asked him, "Son, what has Christ done for us all . . . for you which entitles Him to our love?" He replied, "I don't know. I think Christ has done a great deal for us, but I don't think of anything in particular." Such was the unimpressive start of D.L. Moody, who went on to become the greatest evangelist of the age. It's not who we are that makes us useful to God; it's whose we are.

The idea that every Christian is a missionary is something of a controversial idea. I found out when I said so, and a fellow believer, a missionary, pushed back. This missionary said:

> I'm always a bit uncomfortable when we say we're all missionaries. . . . We really need to emphasize, just as the apostle Paul, we are all witnesses and evangelists wherever we step. A missionary is one who crosses into another culture to witness and evangelize. I feel when we call everybody a missionary, we water down and minimize the cost, the sacrifice, the preparation, and the training needed to surrender one's culture, and, to the best of their ability, incarnate into another's culture for the sake of the Gospel.

These are strong arguments for not saying every Christian is a missionary. To be sure, we do not want to minimize the special call and sacrificial cost the career missionaries make. But doesn't Christ command all his followers to forsake all for his sake and the gospel? We want to honor those who have sacrificed so much to accept the special call. But we can promote the general call without diminishing the special call. In fact, fully embracing the general call will strengthen and support the career missionaries as never before.

Spurgeon clearly believed every Christian is a missionary, as did a number of outstanding Christian leaders, such as J. Christy Wilson, the pioneer missionary to Afghanistan.

On the other hand, many Christian leaders such as John Piper, Patrick Johnstone, and the Gospel Coalition's Elliot Clark argue that every Christian is not a missionary. The reason is that every Christian does not have the special call of, say, an apostle Paul, to go to a distant land and plant churches cross-culturally. They contend that if everyone is missionary, then no one is a missionary.

So, who is correct? Or is there a sense in which both groups are correct? It really all depends on what we mean by "missionary." If we are using the word in its technical sense, of someone called and sent out to plant churches cross-culturally, then clearly everyone is a *not* a missionary. But if we take the word in its more general sense, to mean someone who is sent with the purpose of advancing God's kingdom according to his or her calling and gifts, then every Christian *is* a missionary.

So in relation to the special call, every Christian is not a missionary, but in relation to the general call, every Christian is a missionary. Here's why:

First, as we have seen in the Last Discourse, Jesus reveals he intends to fulfill the Great Commission through his Body, and not through professional missionaries alone. This means the mission of God is an essential part of our identity as Christians.

The Christian faith is not a religion. In *The Life of God in the Soul of Man*, Scottish pastor and theologian Henry Scougal wrote, "True religion is a union of the soul with God, a real participation of the divine nature, the very image of God drawn upon the soul, or, in the apostle's phrase, 'It is Christ formed within us.'"[69]

God brings us not only into his life, but also into his work, the mission of God. Christians are followers of Christ, not merely practitioners of a religious tradition. And God has been pursuing his mission to redeem people from all nations into his kingdom since before the creation and throughout the period in which the Bible was written.[70]

He continues to pursue that mission throughout the Church Age and will continue his mission until the consummation of redemption at the return of Christ. Since the triune God is continuing his redemptive mission, if we are following Christ, we are necessarily part of the mission of God. It is impossible to faithfully follow the one who entrusted us with the Great Commission without doing our part to obey it.

Therefore, being mission-minded is not merely an optional add-on for the professional or the enthusiast only. It is the joy and privilege of every child of God. In this sense, the term "evangelical Christian" is redundant.

Jesus said, "Follow me, and I will make you fishers of men." He also said, "For whoever would save his life will lose it, but whoever loses his life for my sake *and the gospel's* will save it" (Mark 8:35). It is clear that Jesus taught that following him means not only personal devotion to himself but also dedication to his redemptive mission in the world. Following Christ is not merely a matter of personal piety and social responsibility.

While it's technically true that not all Christians are called to be missionaries, I am suggesting that this is probably not the most helpful message to a Church that has, for the most part, lost its sense that the mission is an essential part of our Christian identity.

Case Study:
Dave, American Retiree and Tentmaker

Dave recently retired at age 74. He has done international corporate sales, owned and operated a Mobil gas station, and run a small business doing home repairs and construction. He does local emergency relief work in South Carolina and mentors and disciples Kenyan orphans, assisting in their vocations.

How did you come to faith?

It's a long story, but it starts with my grandmother, Nana, when I was a child. She was a very strong Christian. She was always admonishing me for my arrogance. And she used to read Bible stories to me. And we sang together and so on. While in high school, our family went to Sunday School and I was connected with the Presbyterian Church and their church basketball team. I then attended Westminster College in Western PA, where I was part of a Christian group, and I got connected with the One movement there. However, it clearly did not make much of an impact at that time.

I quit college and spent five months traveling around Europe. On that trip, I walked into the Vatican and it's huge. And you see all this opulence. I walked into the Sistine Chapel. I was practically alone there. To get into the Sistine Chapel today, you need to get a ticket six months in advance to get in for just ten minutes. In 1970, I was lying on the floor of the Sistine Chapel looking at Michelangelo's frescoes. And I was amazed. I was amazed at the art, as well as the opulence.

I started to read different authors, Christian authors, Louis Smedes and Marianne Williamson, who isn't exactly a Christ-follower, but she is a believer in the Lord. There were others, like C.S. Lewis and so on. At that point, I was fifty years old, living in Oregon, working in high-tech. And I started to read the Bible. I couldn't figure out why, but I did. And then, I met Jenifer. She basically said, "If you want to be with me, we're going to church." And I was like, okay, we're going to church. They say it takes eight steps to sell somebody a product, and in a way, I was on step number six when I met Jenifer. And in the first week—all because of Jenifer—I moved to step seven.

With her, the path to step eight was going to Willow Creek Church in Chicago on Wednesday nights and listening to John Ortberg, the Bible teacher. And along with three thousand people at Willow Creek Church, Ortberg's looking right at me. He's looking right at me all the time. After a few weeks, I got to the point where I looked at the mirror and said, "All right, are you willing to bet your entire eternal life on the fact that you're in charge of things, or is there really a God who is charge of things?" And I said, and I mean this, though it may be funny, but I said, "I'm a coward. I'm not going to bet on me." It's Pascal's Wager. You must either believe or not believe. If there is no God and you don't believe, there is no loss. But if there is a God and you don't believe, you've got a problem. The loss is infinite. And if there is a God and you believe, you have infinite, eternal gain. So, looking in the mirror and considering Pascal's Wager and going to church with

Jenifer, I really start to get fired up about listening. And about listening to what Jesus really said, the gospel.

How did you become a businessman?

Well, that's pretty easy. My dad started me with tools when I was a kid. I started working on cars, and although he never did much construction work around the house, he could fix anything. I'm not aware of what he did in the way of building, yet he was always great at repairs, and that's how I learned about tools. Then when I moved to Vermont in my first marriage, we bought a house right off the bat. The house was a two-hundred-year-old farmhouse that was not livable, and we lived in an apartment while I was working for my dad in his lumberyard and hardware business.

And so, I rebuilt the house, and I got some help along the way to do certain things, but I still have scars from hitting myself with a chisel or from electric shocks. I worked for contractors and learned more. Fast forward through my life, I've always fixed things and accumulated tools. Back before I met Jenifer and when I was working for Intel, I bought a house in Phoenix, and I did a lot of work on that. Then eight or nine years later, when I moved to Chicago with Jenifer, and even though I was in high tech, I was still taking on projects around the neighborhood because I love doing that work. It's just, God made me to be able to think and use tools and do what I call "entrepreneurial engineering." If you don't have a hammer but you have a chisel, you have a hammer. If you don't have a hammer but you've got an iron bar, you have a hammer.

And I met a couple of people along the way at the gas station who said, "Dave, you can do more." I always had a hankering for international work. I had gone to Paris on a school trip in my junior year of high school. So, I quit college and went to Europe on the five-month trip. In my first marriage, Carol and I quit our jobs, and we went to Europe for three months, skiing and traveling around Europe. And I just loved international travel, particularly in Europe.

But thirteen years later, I decided I wanted more. With great selfishness, I decided to leave my family and go to graduate school in Phoenix. I got into Thunderbird International Graduate School because I wanted to study and do something internationally. And of course, that ended up being sales and marketing and so on. And then right out of that college, I went to work for Intel.

How do you use your vocation in the Lord's mission?

Well, you take all those skills, and you determine what the needs are or what the problems are. And I saw the problem with the guys from the orphanage. Number one happens when they graduated from high school and they were admitted to college. In the Kenyan system, you get into college based on your examination results. So, depending on your examination results, two things can happen. One, you can go to a good school, or two, you can enter a program that allows you to only go to the first level, which is what they call the artisan level. So, you go one year for the artisan level of electrical engineering to be an electrician. And that's as far as you can go for two reasons. But the orphanage wouldn't pay for them, and there was a need there that we might be able to fill.

As they got admitted to college at whatever level, the orphanage would literally drive them to college, drop them off at the front gate, and drive away. There was no setup and no follow-up. They had a room to go to, and they had their classes to go to, but they had to figure everything else out on their own. The room that they went to was basically a college dormitory with no bed and no furniture whatsoever. The orphanage gave them a mat and a blanket. And if they went to cold regions, they got a coat. And that's it.

I get so excited about it because it's just so cool to see them now, when I went over this past December. One of the donors to Joystone that's giving money to one of these kids is a whole church in Summerton, SC. This is a congregation of 150 people giving $1,500 a year for Moses, to get his 15,000 shillings a month so he can pay his rent and eat. But he's taking money out of his pocket, out of that upkeep, and helping another kid in his college. On the other hand, I've been really harsh on "Hey, Mr. Dave, I'm out of money. I need more money." I said, did you get the 15,000 at the beginning of the month? Yes. What did you do with it? Do you have your cell phone? Yes. We gave you the cell phone. You better take care of it. Because if you drop it in the toilet and you need another one, yo-yo. You know what yo-yo, means? You're on your own.

What motivates you to do what you are doing in the mission?

One answer is I'm the same age as a lot of guys here on the South Carolina island where Jenifer and I have been living for the past nineteen years. They've decided that after their forty-year career, they deserve to do nothing but play golf and give a donation to the church.

Now, that's not to say that a lot of people don't donate to "Second Helpings" or to the church in some way or another. There are a lot of good Christians—Evangelicals, Presbyterians, and Catholics here on the island. But I still go back to: Who will go for me? And I say send me.

What advice would you give to other people, especially businesspeople who are retirees?

I think you've got to search your heart. And you have to understand that God commanded us to go. To go. While we're doing this work, particularly the Compassion Action Team stuff, you're going to get an opportunity to preach the gospel, to talk about your life with Christ, to talk about why your eternal soul is in question until you believe. You have to search your soul as a retired businessman or a thirty-year-old person working in an office. You search your soul and say, Am I a Christian? Am I a dedicated Christian? Go listen to the sermons of Tim Keller in his "Gospel in Life" podcasts for three sermons and figure that out. Search your soul and say: What can I do?

Go to your pastor or go to any church and say I just committed to Christ and then go figure out how to use your skill set, what you can do. There are accountants who can do pro bono work for indigent people who don't know how to do their taxes. I don't care what your profession is or what your skill set is. God gives you those gifts to use for the Kingdom and to bring people along and be the light on the hill. And there's a multiplication effect. You do that and people will see you doing that.

> And you get so much out of it. I mean, I get such a charge from these kids, in watching them help each other or planning for what they're going to do in the vacation time. So, what advice would I give to others? In your line of work or any line of work, you have to make the decision that, as a Christian, after you commit, your job is to serve.

QUESTIONS FOR REFLECTION AND DISCUSSION

1. Do you feel that part of following Christ is being a witness for him?

2. How can people who are not outgoing and who don't have a gift for evangelism be part of the mission?

Chapter 10

The Higher Purpose of Your Vocation

> [Work] should be looked upon, not as a necessary drudgery to be undergone for the purpose of making money, but as a way of life in which the nature of man should find its proper exercise and delight and so fulfill itself to the glory of God.
> —Dorothy Sayers

Working as a fast-food worker doesn't seem to lend itself to being a witness for Christ. But the way one woman served her customers stood out. Pastor Adam Weatherly tells this story about stopping at a fast-food restaurant. The lady who served his family was very attentive and had a big smile on her face. He recalled:

> After we finished our lunch, we started cleaning up to leave. At that moment, I started feeling the Holy Spirit tugging at me to go pray for her. So I got up from my seat and walked to the side door that led to where she was standing behind

the counter. "Yes Sir, can I help you with anything else?" the lady kindly asked.

"No ma'am," I said. "What is your name?"

"My name is Jenn," she replied.

"Jenn, it's nice to meet you. My name is Adam. This may sound kinda weird to you, but I'm a pastor and I feel like I'm supposed to pray for you today." I expressed to her.

Suddenly, the Holy Spirit nudged me to tell her, "The work you are doing and the good attitude you have here is not going unnoticed."

"Jenn, is it okay for me to pray with you?" I asked.

With a stunned look, she said, "Yes, please. That would be nice."

"Is there anything specific that I can pray with you today about?" I asked.

For the next few moments, Jenn poured her heart out to me. She told me about how she had walked away from church ten years ago when her husband walked out on her and her four children. Over the years, she had made bad choices in relationships and life. Her life sounded rough.

Without any prompting from me about church Jenn divulged, "I was born and raised in the church. I know that I have moved away from God, and now I feel like he has been calling me to go back. I've been debating on whether I should go back or not."

Then she told me how she feels that God has been providing a way for her to get back to church. The tires on her car split over a week ago. Since then, two different customers have given her a one-hundred-dollar tip to purchase new tires for her car.

"I can't help but believe that God is up to something in my life now. Because God has not only sent the two customers with the money for my car, but because He also asked you to pray with me. I can't deny it anymore, I'm supposed to be back in church," she uttered as tears filled her eyes.

In God's economy, work is not just a means to an end. We don't get a job just to make money and elevate our status. Work is a calling from God, a sacred vocation. Tim Keller suggests the biblical idea of work is "the gracious expression of creative energy in the service of others."[71]

The motivation comes from a desire to please God and serve others in love. The specific kinds of work we choose will be guided by our passions, gifts, and abilities and by the needs of those we serve, if we are fortunate enough to be able to choose. And given the general call to the mission of God, we can integrate into our work ways to share the gospel as well as demonstrate it by our love and faithfulness.

This vision of work fits with what the Bible teaches about every believer being a priest:

> As you come to him, a living stone rejected by men but in the sight of God chosen and precious, you yourselves like living stones are being built up as a spiritual house, to be a holy priesthood, to offer spiritual sacrifices acceptable to God through Jesus Christ . . . you are a chosen race, a royal priesthood, a holy nation, a people for his own possession, that you may proclaim the excellencies of him who called you out of darkness into his marvelous light. (I Peter 2:4–5, 9)

In this vision, we are priests not in order to mediate, but to draw attention to the Mediator "that we may proclaim the excellencies of him who called you."

God is sovereign over everything:

> In him we have obtained an inheritance, having been predestined according to the purpose of him who works all things according to the counsel of his will. (Ephesians 1:11)

So, the work we do, our vocations, are not randomly determined ways of earning a living. God places us where we are as teachers, or lawyers, or plumbers, or maintenance workers for his purposes—not merely to do the work well, but also to glorify him and advance his kingdom in the process.

Case Study: Steve, American Doctor and Tentmaker

Steve is an emergency room physician who uses his vocation to serve the Lord on various short-term missions. He goes on several missions each year, using his skills as a physician to partner with Christian organizations and local churches on the ground and to help provide medical care and relief in the Lord's name.

How did you come to faith?

I was fortunate enough to be brought up in a Christian family. I never had any of those moments when the sky parted on the road to Damascus. It wasn't any one time. Sunday was always a day for church and family.

My cousins would be there. Both sides of my grandparents were heavily involved in church. On my mother's side, my grandparents were sextons of a church, so they lived right on the church grounds to take care of the maintenance. So when we would go to Grandma's and Grandpa's house, we were going to church.

The cousins all lived in the area, thirteen cousins on that side. Mother had two sisters and a brother. Everybody was in the area. It was always nice to see everybody, and we would make a day of it until early afternoon.

My uncle was a Bishop in the Mennonite church. My grandparents were very faithful. They said my grandfather went to church for over fifty years without ever missing a Sunday. Later on in life, I asked him, "Grandpa, how and why did you do that?" He said, "It wasn't out of commitment. It's just where I wanted to be." That's always stuck with me because where else would I want to be other than worshipping on Sunday? They were very much a "plain family," as you would call them in that area. They didn't take vacations other than they might take a day and drive somewhere. Or, they might work five and a half days a week, working on Saturdays 'til noon time. And you might take off a day sometime in the summer to do something. That's the mentality my father grew up with.

I saw the love of Jesus in my parents. I saw how they interacted with others, their priorities in life. When you're young, you don't always understand that. But when you start getting older, you see your friends and how their parents would act. They were so different in so many ways.

We would pray together as a family every night and, of course, at every meal. At night we would all get together and pray. And I knew by that time, even before I went through confirmation class and baptism, that I wanted what they had in Jesus. There was nowhere else I wanted to be. If I can be like that, I will be fortunate in life. So I never had any one moment that I could say, "This was the day that I came to faith." It was a gradual journey and I knew where I wanted to be and got to receive that. I asked Jesus into my life before I even went through the confirmation classes and had a public confession and baptism. That's how it was.

How did you become a doctor?

Growing up, my mother was a nurse. She would have to work an occasional weekend, maybe once a month, and we would always go into the hospital either on a Saturday or Sunday if she was working. We would either have lunch with her, or if she was working the evening shift, we'd have dinner. I always felt comfortable in a hospital. It was kind of an odd thing, if I look back at it. Most people aren't comfortable going into a hospital. They'd rather not be there, but I thought wow, this is really nice. I liked being there. I liked not just visiting my mother but being in that setting. It seemed like a good place for me to be.

Both my grandmothers died from cancer. And this angered me a little bit. Why did they have to die when I was twelve years old? But it also motivated me to understand cancer. And what can I do about this at some point in my life? When I was in college, I had a summer job as an orderly.

I went to Moravian College, and one of my roommates in college was my best friend. He organized mission trips to Haiti. He was Catholic, and one of his priests was affiliated with a mission down in Haiti. And it always made me wonder, Why do you want to spend your summer going down to Haiti for two weeks? I had to work so I never went with them. And this was certainly a bit of a regret at the time, but I got to focus on, "Wow, this is what people do—leave the country for a two-week mission."

[In medical school] I took out loans for the first two years, and then in my second year I found a National Health Corps scholarship. They paid for all the tuition and gave me room and board and a stipend for the books and supplies. And when I graduated, I served with the Indian Health Service with the Cherokee tribe in Oklahoma.

While I was in Oklahoma, I went to a Baptist church. I had never been in a Baptist church before, and the first time we went, I saw they had a praise band. I had never seen that before. We don't have drums and guitars on the Moravian side or on the Brethren/Mennonite side. You didn't have any instruments, and that was certainly eye-opening. I thought, Wow, this is really great. People are happy, clapping. This is what should happen in worship. So, it was a great time to also grow in faith when I went there.

Colossians 3:23–24 says, "Whatever you do, work heartily, as for the Lord and not for men, knowing that from the Lord you will receive the inheritance as your reward. You are serving the Lord Christ."

What motivates you to do your work?

What am I doing? Am I doing it for the glory of the Lord or am I doing it for my own glory? And sometimes in the hospital it's a little bit of a challenge. Am I showing the hope and love of Jesus with my interactions with others at work? I'm tested at times. Sometimes in the

Emergency Room, you have the belligerent, intoxicated patient. You have the person who is strung out on drugs, who refuses to do anything. And he may say some very unkind words to you and the rest of the staff. We have a patient who even now comes in with kidney problems and won't go to dialysis and then wants us to fix him. And you want to say, "Come on, buddy. You've got to take some personal responsibility." But then, am I showing the love and hope of Jesus?

And I have to say, you know, I wasn't always that way. There was a time period after I got out of the Indian Health Service. I came back and worked in Lancaster in a kind of dream job. It was a private group, very busy and very lucrative. I made partner after two years. The money was very good. And then I kind of was going wayward at times, when I was starting to work for myself and for the almighty dollar and what I could get out of it. Was I looking at the next big vacation adventure that I could take my family on? Am I looking at another property? What's motivating me now? On the outside, yes, I would never admit that I wasn't a Christian, but I know I wasn't acting that way. I would go on a mission trip once a year with a co-worker down to Mexico. So I was thinking, Hey, I'm doing all right, I'm going for a week. We technically didn't have any vacation. So if you took a week off, you still worked the same amount of shifts. And after twelve years, I knew I was heading in the wrong direction. My kids wanted to play sports on Sunday instead of going to church. Okay, that's fine. They'll go next week.

Maybe I can pick up an extra day at work and make some more money instead of going to church. It got to the point where I was getting close to being divorced from my wife because I wasn't paying attention to her. I would go off and do other things that I thought were more fun. I had a friend I always looked up to as part of a men's group that I had attended. I hadn't attended for about three years. I said, "Tom, hey, you know, one time in men's group, you talked about your wife saying she's going to walk out on you because of the way you were acting." I said, "I'm at that point in life. Can I talk to you?"

I didn't want to give up what I had. I thought, Wow, you know, I'm not going to get another job like this. This is my dream job. Why am I even thinking about this? The Lord brought some conviction—it's time to leave. There were other things occurring. Where I should be? I need to leave that environment. And I took another leap of faith in my life.

I had been a partner in a private group. The remuneration was very, very good. So I became an employee at another group in the area. I found out that I could take more than one week of vacation. I've come to understand I don't need those extra dollars. I don't need those extra things in life because they're not important. And that I'll give up money to serve the Lord. And at that time, I started getting involved with other organizations, mission organizations. And another motivation is I love working with other Christians and being inspired by doing a lot of the group trips as well as the individual trips to mission hospitals. I like to hear other people's stories and where they're at, and it certainly does inspire me.

So how do you use your vocation to serve the Lord?

I've always kind of felt I had a gift or calling for international and cross-cultural missions, and that started in college when I was exposed to friends from Tanzania. It seemed I could easily connect with others, and I had an interest in different cultures and different lands. I hadn't traveled anywhere outside the country up until that one time I went to Honduras the first time. And after I came back, I was like, Wow, I really like the Central American culture. Where else can I go?

So how do I use medicine? Providing physical and emotional support opens up the doors to sharing the gospel. I can use my emergency medicine skills to help people with no expectation of any personal gain. And a lot of times with the emergency medicine, you know a little bit about a lot of things. You're not a specialist in any one field of medicine other than the ER, so you understand how to manage people with high blood pressure and diabetes. You can take care of people with colds and pneumonias, things like that, and that helps when going to mission hospitals. If I'll step out of my comfort zone to do those types of things, I can work on the wards and manage patients. And a lot of times you get the question, "Why did you come?" Why? Why did I come to this other country? Sometimes people there will think you're being paid by the church, the government, or your job back home. And when you get to share why you came, especially in the Muslim countries, it is the best time. Well, it's because of Jesus.

One time always stands out to me. We were building wheelchairs in Jericho, in the West Bank. And we had wheelchairs sent over. We're working with a local organization there, a Christian organization. And a father brought his daughter, who had pretty bad cerebral palsy. It was a challenging case for the physical therapist and the people making this wheelchair because she was a bit contorted and certainly not your average person in a wheelchair.

It took some time. This young girl was six or seven. People spent time with her, playing on the mats, interacting with her, even though they couldn't speak the language. And the father was very standoffish at first. He knew we were a Christian organization. We finished and he went over to one translator and said, "Why are these people coming? Why do you people do what you do?" So? "Because we want to serve."

He said, "I went to the local mosque. The imam there gave me ten shekels and said, 'Go on your way.' I went to another one and they gave me fifteen shekels and said go on your way. But I came here and these people all treated her like she was their own daughter. I don't know much about your Jesus, but he certainly taught you how to love." So when you have that opportunity, you know you're planting a seed and you're doing it for no gain of your own. It's only for the glory of the Lord. So I get to use those skills to do that, and that's very, very rewarding. Then, when I go to disasters or low-resource areas, emergency medicine always comes into play. You're dealing with broken legs, bruises. And you certainly can utilize the talents and knowledge gained over the years.

What advice would you give someone for using their healthcare vocation for the mission?

Certainly the first step is to pray about it. What's your motivation? Is it because you want to travel to some foreign land? Well, I'd suggest you go on vacation instead. What are your skill sets? Look, look at what you can do or what you are willing to do.

Medicine has become so specialized that sometimes we're scared to go off and do things that we know we can do but can't do here because insurance might not allow me to do that. There's somebody who's smarter or more specialized, so I better defer to him or her. But you'd be amazed at what you can accomplish if you let the Lord lead you.

How much time can you devote? Can you go for a week? Can you go for two weeks? Are you looking at going for two years? All those kind of things you have to look at. I'd say get your feet wet with one short trip. Maybe even look at somewhere locally. I got to work at a homeless center. They had a medical clinic. That was always very rewarding also.

After that, decide about different trips. What do I like? Where do I seem to be a benefit for the Lord? Talk to others. I think you can gain a lot of knowledge and you'd be surprised at how many doors start opening up when you do that. There are multiple conferences for medical missions that you can attend.

Questions for Reflection and Discussion

1. What kinds of work most easily lend themselves to being a witness for Christ?

2. What kinds of vocations are the most challenging for Christians who want to be a witness for Christ in them? How can they overcome the challenges?

3. What are some of the pitfalls of serving as a "tentmaker," or self-supporting witness for Christ?

PART FOUR

APPLICATIONS

Imagine God's People pouring their lives and resources into the advancing Kingdom!

—Richard Lovelace

CHAPTER 11

THE PROBLEM OF EVIL, GOD'S SOVEREIGNTY, AND THE ADVANCE OF THE GOSPEL

> There is no neutral ground in the universe. Every square inch, every split second, is claimed by God and counterclaimed by Satan.
> —C.S. LEWIS

THE POWERFUL BACK TO JERUSALEM mission vision of China's house church movement almost died out during the severe persecution of the Cultural Revolution (1966–76). Even before that, many missionaries from the three main groups of house churches were prevented from working through imprisonment and being put to forced hard labor. Many died. One of the few who survived was Simon Zao, who managed to emerge after forty years of imprisonment, beatings, and torture. He would become the link to revive the Back to Jerusalem movement, now working in the 10/40 window.

Satan's Rebellion and Defeat

Before we consider how individuals and churches can apply Jesus' vision for his mission, it is helpful to consider the larger context of the unfolding cosmic spiritual battle. In his redemptive plan, God resolves the problem of evil. The context for God's mission is the revolt of the forces of evil against the holy God and his Kingdom. The marvel is how God sovereignly uses all things, even the evil things and the disasters of the world, for his good purposes.

The Bible does not give a full account of Satan's rebellion. We know that he was once an angel in heaven called Lucifer, but led a rebellion against God, taking one-third of the angels with him.

God said of him:

> Your heart was proud because of your beauty;
>   you corrupted your wisdom for the sake of your splendor.
> I cast you to the ground. (Ezekiel 28:14-17)

Satan continues to war against God and his people but he, along with his allied powers, is defeated, doomed, and, in the end, will be destroyed (Revelation 12:7-9, 20:7-10).

The Origin and Nature of Evil

When God created beings with volition, or the ability to exercise will, it meant such beings could, at least in theory, chose to turn their wills against his good and holy will. The possibility of evil is inherent in freedom.

So it was with the devil. As Lucifer, he was a highly exalted angel. As a pure spirit, he would not be tempted to commit the sins of the flesh, but as Ezekiel reveals, he fell to the sin of pride, choosing to love his own splendor above the glory of the one who bestowed it on him:

You said in your heart,

> 'I will ascend to heaven;
> above the stars of God.' (Isaiah 14:13)

Lucifer's tragic sin was to try to take the place of God, and so he fell from his created perfection into the misery of utter, irredeemable corruption. And in the garden, he tempted man to that same perilous quest.

> He said to the woman, "Did God actually say, 'You shall not eat of any tree in the garden'?" And the woman said to the serpent, "We may eat of the fruit of the trees in the garden, but God said, 'You shall not eat of the fruit of the tree that is in the midst of the garden, neither shall you touch it, lest you die.' " (Genesis 3:1–30)

Notice Satan tempts our first parents to the same vain, idolatrous quest that brought him down: "You will be like God." He introduces the idea of exalting self as an object of worship. At the same time, he blasphemously slanders the character of God in three ways. First, he sows doubt about God's word and character: "Did God really say . . ."

> But the serpent said to the woman, "You will not surely die. For God knows that when you eat of it your eyes will be opened, and you will be like God, knowing good and evil." So when the woman saw that the tree was good for food, and that it was a delight to the eyes, and that the tree was to be desired to make one wise, she took of its fruit and ate, and she also gave some to her

husband who was with her, and he ate. Then the eyes of both were opened, and they knew that they were naked. And they sewed fig leaves together and made themselves loincloths. (Genesis 3:4–7)

Second, the Father of lies makes God out to be a liar by flatly contradicting him: "You will not surely die." And finally, he promises a benefit of becoming like God: "Your eyes will be opened, and you will be like God, knowing good and evil."

Here is the origin of evil in the world. Satan propagated a false narrative designed to destroy man's relationship with God and enslave him in his own kingdom of darkness. In doing so, he usurps authority over man, and brings about Adam's death. The Bible rightly calls Satan a liar, a murderer, and a thief (John 8:44). Satan's devices include the false narrative, temptation, and accusation. God counters them through a revelation of the truth, deliverance, and forgiveness.

The fall of the entire human race in our first parents sets the stage for the mission of God. When God pronounced his just punishment on Satan and humanity, he also revealed something of his redemptive mission.

When our first parents fell from their created perfection into corruption, the entire human race fell with them. The woman would be subjected to pain in childbirth and conflict with her husband, and the man would be subject to toil, futility, and death (3:17–19).

But when God curses the serpent Satan, he says:

> "I will put enmity between you and the woman,
>   and between your offspring and her offspring;
> he shall bruise your head,
>   and you shall bruise his heel." (Genesis 3:15)

Pointing to the cross, Satan will deliver a non-fatal blow against the Messiah; but the Son of God will utterly destroy the devil, initially through the cross and ultimately in the consummation of redemption.

The larger context of God's great redemptive plan is this battle between good and evil. The outcome could never be in doubt. A rebellious, finite, fallible, fallen angel who is, as a creature, dependent on the Almighty is utterly outmatched by the perfect, infinite, self-sufficient, omnipotent, omniscient, sovereign Creator and Redeemer. God's mission is not merely to redeem a people for himself out of ruined humanity; it is also to forever quell the rebellion of the angelic band and its allies who made the ultimate tragic error of judgment. They chose the way of self-love over worshipping the only one worthy of worship—the infinitely great, infinitely good creator-redeemer God.

Through the work of Jesus Christ on the cross, God not only saves sinners. He also reveals his glory, vindicates his honor, and resolves the problem of evil. The redeemed will be saved from sin and its just penalty, and those who refuse the free offer of God's forgiveness and grace will be forever excluded from God's kingdom. The Enemy and those who are allied with him will be justly consigned to the place of eternal punishment. In this way, God upholds and fully restores the moral order of the universe.

The greatest foreshadowing of this ultimate triumph is the fact that God used Satan's best shot—his use of Judas to bring about the death of the Messiah—as the primary means of resolving the problem of evil and sealing Satan's own eternal doom. Satan taking on God is something like a rat taking on a lion, except that the distance between a rat and a lion is finite, but the distance between Satan and God is infinite.

How God Resolves the Problem of Evil

God's mission is not only to reclaim the nations he created for himself, it is to vindicate his good name. He does so by destroying the devil's false narrative at its root. Satan blasphemously insinuated that God was somehow holding out on Adam, could not be trusted, and that there was a better way—the way of self-realization through forsaking the living God for worthless idols. Initially, this meant forsaking God for the sake of independently acquiring the fruit of the knowledge of good and evil.

God utterly refutes this damnable false narrative through his ultimate self-revelation in the life, death, and resurrection of the Lord Jesus Christ. Satan claimed God was somehow "holding out" on man; God gave his only Son. Satan cast doubt on God's character; God revealed his blinding infinite moral perfection by sending a Savior who would save sinners without compromising the righteous requirements of the law. Satan talked up the way of rebellion and self-realization as the way to be like God; God revealed that Jesus Christ alone is the way, the truth, and the life. Satan offers the false promise of godlikeness to the unbeliever; Jesus delivers the actual promise of godliness to the believer.

And just as God used Satan's attack against the Savior for the devil's own undoing and the ultimate good of those appointed to eternal life, he continues to use evil and trials for the good of his people and the glory of his name.

We see this, for example, in the life of Joseph. Joseph's brothers tried to kill him, but their very effort to do so ultimately led not only to Israel's salvation in Egypt but also to our own. ". . . You meant evil against me, but God meant it for good, to bring it about that many people should be kept alive" (Genesis 50:20).

God promises this kind of sovereign reversal for his people: "And we know that for those who love God all things work together for good, for those who are called according to his purpose" (Romans 8:28).

How God Uses Evil Events for Good

In his first sermon, America's great theologian Jonathan Edwards summed up how God sovereignly uses everything for the good of those he loves:

> Our bad things turn out for good.
>
> Our good things can never be taken away.
>
> The best is yet to come.[72]

God also sovereignly uses the great disasters of the world for his good purposes. Notice carefully the words of Jesus: "And when you hear of wars and rumors of wars, do not be alarmed. This must take place, but the end is not yet. For nation will rise against nation, and kingdom against kingdom. There will be earthquakes in various places; there will be famines. These are but the beginning of the birth pains" (Mark 13:7–8).

I saw something of this dynamic in 2010, when the Lord led me to go on a mission trip to a closed Middle Eastern country. Evangelism was illegal in that country. He very clearly impressed on me the well-known story of Joshua circling Jericho for seven days on me in relation to this trip. I didn't know exactly what to expect but I went expecting the Lord to do something. A group of about twelve of us drove throughout the entire country for seven days, just praying that God would open up the country for the gospel, trusting he would since we were praying for something we knew was in accordance with his will. I thought that maybe one day, there would be a change in government, and missionaries would be allowed in. But God answered in a most powerful and unexpected way. Ten weeks later, the Arab Spring, a great series of uprisings, came, and at least two million people would migrate from the region in the first year alone, often into countries where they could freely hear the gospel and Christians.[73]

These prayers had unusual power because the Lord had very clearly led us to go and because we were praying for something he had purposed. I felt that God was, in a sense, pulling back the curtain to show us that the Arab Spring was not simply random political upheaval but that God was sovereignly working out his redemptive purposes for many who lived under governments that denied them free access to the only way of salvation.

Jesus doesn't just say these things will take place; he says they *must* take place. Somehow, in God's economy, disasters such as conflicts, wars, earthquakes, famines, and the like are necessary in a fallen world that is being redeemed. We can speculate about why this might be. Is God not weaning us from all the things that might lull us into a false sense of security? We can and will lose every temporal prop so that we can find the greater good. Some may only receive the gospel through "transformative learning," the deep, structural shift in basic assumptions that typically results from the trauma and suffering.[74] Some will only turn to God when the comforts and blessings of a settled life are taken away. We know this happens.

As of this writing, as the war between Russia and Ukraine continues, a Romanian missionary who ministers on the front lines reported there were some local moves of God for a time among troops on the front lines. Another missionary couple who work among the earthquake victims in southern Turkey also reported an unprecedented move of God in the region. Their small church has quadrupled in size in the past year. Similarly, Taysir "Tass" Abu Saada, a former aide to the late Palestinian leader Yasser Arafat, recently told CBN News that God's Holy Spirit is already changing Palestinian hearts through dreams and visions. He reports that two hundred Gazans came to faith in Christ in early 2024.[75] He is convinced this is only the beginning of a move of God. Similarly, a mission board in Lebanon is reporting a revival has started in 2025 in that country which has suffered a political and economic collapse in recent years.

God sees to it that temporal blessings leave us wanting in order to position us to receive the greater eternal blessing. "For the creation was subjected to futility, not willingly, but because of him who subjected it, in hope that the creation itself will be set free from its bondage to corruption and obtain the freedom of the glory of the children of God" (Romans 8:20–21).

Questions for Reflection and Discussion

1. If Jesus has resolved the problem of evil, why is there still so much evil and suffering in the world?

2. Why is having a "theology of suffering" helpful to believers in working through the trials and problems of life?

3. What are some ways God might use the most difficult trials people face for the greater good?

4. In what way might tests of adversity ultimately be less difficult than tests of prosperity?

Chapter 12

Praying Together for Revival and Reformation

> God is not a reluctant giver, but he will not give such a precious gift as the Holy Spirit to seekers and non-seekers alike.
> —J. Rodman Williams

I mentioned previously that I was part of a group of men who prayed weekly for revival for some years before the outpouring of the Holy Spirit in Toronto in 1994. A local pediatrician partnered with a pastor to host the meeting at a conveniently located hotel. Looking back, a number of the local church pastors saw a surge of members in their churches at that time.

Sometimes we underestimate the power of prayer offered in simple faith. Irene Webster-Smith was a missionary who started an orphanage for Japanese girls. She led them all to Christ.

One evening they read Mark 11:22–24 for their devotions. Here Jesus said, "I tell you the truth, if anyone says to this mountain, 'Go, throw yourself into the sea,' and does not doubt in his heart but believes that what he says will happen, it will be done for him."

One little girl asked, "Teacher, did Jesus really mean what he said?" Webster-Smith replied, "Of course, why do you ask?"

The child went on to say, "There is a large mountain between Sunrise Orphanage and the Sea of Japan. If this were removed, we would have a beautiful view of the sea."

This was too much for the missionary, so she went on to explain that Jesus didn't necessarily mean a physical mountain, but that if we had difficulties, he would remove them. The little girl would not be deterred and said, "Jesus must have been talking about a real mountain because he said *this* mountain. I'm going to ask him to take it away."

Not long after this, bulldozers appeared on the mountain. The Japanese Government had decided to use it for fill to reclaim land in a shallow area of the sea.[76]

ZECHARIAH FORETELLS UNITED, EXTRAORDINARY PRAYER FOR REVIVAL

God not only promises and commands revival, he foretells a great global awakening with an unprecedented gathering of the nations in the book of Zechariah:

> "The inhabitants of one city shall go to another, saying, 'Let us go at once to entreat the favor of the Lord and to seek the Lord of hosts; I myself am going.' Many peoples and strong nations shall come to seek the Lord . . . ten men from the nations of every tongue shall take

hold of the robe of a Jew, saying, 'Let us go with you, for we have heard that God is with you.'" (Zechariah 8:20–23)

Zechariah's prophecy inspired the great theologian of revival, Jonathan Edwards, to write a famous book on the subject. In the manner of the day, the very long title summarizes the entire book:

> *A Humble Attempt to Promote Explicit Agreement and Visible Union of God's People in Extraordinary Prayer for the Revival of Religion and the Advancement of Christ's Kingdom on Earth, Pursuant to Scripture-Promises and Prophecies Concerning the Last Time.*

Edwards, the leader of the American Great Awakening (1727–50), published *A Humble Attempt* in 1747. This fruit of the First Great Awakening was instrumental in leading to the prayer movements that preceded the Second Great Awakening (1780–1810).

Forty years after its publication, in 1784, a Scottish pastor sent a copy of *A Humble Attempt* to Baptist leaders in England, including Andrew Fuller, John Ryland, and John Sutcliffe. They reprinted the book and met monthly to pray for revival and the advance of the gospel. It was from this group that William Carey was raised up to launch the modern Protestant missions movement which started in the 1790s.[77]

In Zechariah's prophecy, two interrelated things are in view. First, Zechariah foresees God pouring out a spirit of prayer and supplication, leading to a united, extraordinary prayer for revival. The prayer is extraordinary because the object of the prayer is God himself. These people are passionately pursuing the greatest good, not the lesser things, the gifts of God. They "seek the Lord of Hosts." They have the urgency of those who will not be denied. This is prevailing prayer: "You will seek me and find me, when you seek me with all your heart" (Jeremiah 29:13).

A Global Great Awakening and Completing the Task of World Evangelization

Our most potent prayers are for the things God has foretold, commanded, and promised—the things he leads us to pray for. When we have a strong biblical warrant for our requests, they will not be denied if we do not give up. Here is the promise of a global great awakening. Zechariah says, "Many peoples and strong nations shall seek the Lord."

The promise is that the elect from all nations will pour into his kingdom as we ask for this move of God. It is clear that God is moving in an extraordinary way because people of all nations are actively seeking the Lord. In my experience of tracking social media evangelism and the use of this medium to engage people with Jesus and the gospel, today often only 1 to 3% of the prayer requests pertain to God and faith; 32% pertain to jobs/finance, and another 32% typically pertain to relationships. But when the Holy Spirit moves in power, the interest in spiritual things increases dramatically.

How can we tell this prophecy refers to all nations? The text says, "Ten men from the nations . . . shall take hold of the robe of a Jew." In the Bible, the word ten is a number of completion.[78] Furthermore, Zechariah speaks of "ten men from the nations of *every* tongue." He doesn't just speak of men from the nations of some tongues or even many tongues. The people of *every* tongue, tribe, and nation are envisioned coming into the kingdom here.

GOD WILL GIVE THE AWAKENING HE HAS PROMISED TO GIVE

As we have said, the mission is God's mission. And the problem of apathy and neglect is of such a magnitude that only God himself can bring about the needed reformation. Patrick Johnstone puts it this way:

> The marginalization of mission has become a part of our Christian thinking, teaching, acting . . . It will take a mighty act of the Holy Spirit to reveal the truth and dispel the blindness because this strikes at the heart of so much of the modern Christian worldview. The vision must be restored to the Church.[79]

Our most effectual prayers are those for which we have a warrant, either through a biblical promise or a prophetic word. In other words, when God specifically leads us to pray, he will surely not withhold from us what he has promised and foretold. We need only ask and be serious about asking.

The promise of revival is clear in scripture. Jesus encourages us to believe God is happy to grant revival to his people if they ask: "If you then, being evil, know how to give good gifts to your children, how much more will your heavenly Father give the Holy Spirit to those who ask Him!" (Luke 11:13)

God not only promises revival if we ask, he commands it:

> "Awake, O sleeper,
>   and arise from the dead,
>   and Christ will shine on you."

> Look carefully then how you walk, not as unwise but as wise, making the best use of the time, because the days are evil. Therefore do not be foolish, but understand what the will of the Lord is. And do not get drunk with wine, for that is debauchery, but be filled with the Spirit (Ephesians 5:14–18)

Jonathan Edwards, perhaps America's greatest authority on revival and her greatest theologian, pointed out that no such great awakening had ever been seen either in Israel or in the history of the Church in his *Humble Attempt*.[80] As is common among the Jewish prophets, Zechariah speaks of both nearer events to come in ancient Israel and looks further ahead to events in church history.

Some have interpreted this as a prophecy about the outpouring of the Spirit at Pentecost (Acts 2:1–41). But this prophecy refers to "the nations of every tongue," i.e., the Gentiles of every nation, so it cannot merely refer to Pentecost, at which the Spirit came upon "Jews, devout men from every nation under heaven" (Acts 2:5). Pentecost may have anticipated the great global awakening in view here, but it cannot be its complete fulfillment. It is only the fulfillment in miniature. Furthermore, what is pictured here is beyond ordinary revival and evangelism. In revival, the Church is awakened, and in evangelism, the evangelist seeks out the unconverted, but in this passage, the nations take the initiative to seek out God's people in order to find the living God.

As mentioned, Edwards emphasizes that this is a prayer for revival since the seekers are not simply asking God for something—they seek God himself:

> Scripture says, "They shall go to pray before the Lord, and to seek the Lord of Hosts." The good that they seek for is

"The Lord of Hosts," Himself. If "seeking God" means no more than seeking the favor or mercy of God then "praying before the Lord" and "seeking the Lord of Hosts" must be looked upon as synonymous. However, "seeking the Lord" is commonly used to mean something far more than seeking something from God. Surely it implies that God Himself is what is desired and sought after.

Thus, the Psalmist desired God, thirsted after Him, and sought after Him:

O God, thou art my God; early will I seek thee. My flesh longeth for thee, in a dry and thirsty land, where no water is, to see thy power and thy glory, so as I have seen thee in the sanctuary. . . . My soul followeth hard after thee. . . . Whom have I in heaven but thee? And there is none upon earth that I desire besides thee.[81]

The prayer is for revival. The result is people of all nations who do not know God will be powerfully motivated to seek the Lord. When God moves in this way, evangelism is no longer an impossibly difficult task. It is like collecting apples that readily fall off the tree.

I caught a small glimpse of what this might be like many years ago. At the time, I attended an international church, a church for people of different countries. One day I bought two small Tabriz rugs from the large Persian rug store in our neighborhood. I had with me a gospel in Dari, which is essentially the same as Farsi, and I gave it to the salesman. This gospel had been translated by a blind Afghan martyr. A few of us from the international church decided to have a potluck dinner at our home, and invite friends from other countries. I invited the salesman.

He came to our house a half hour early and poured out his story to me. He had been the chief of police in Tehran before the Islamic

Revolution of 1979. Since he was part of the old regime, he was thrown in jail and his home was looted. Eventually he and his family fled to America, where he ended up working as the sales manager in a local Persian rug store. Because he had lost everything, he still felt traumatized, even though this was several years after the revolution.

At the end of his sad tale, he announced he wanted to become a Christian. When he had started to read the gospel, he felt the peace of God come over him as the Holy Spirit moved in his heart in a mysterious way. No evangelism was needed as he sought me out and asked to become a Christian. All I had to do was explain the gospel and invite him to repent of his sins and receive Christ as Savior and Lord. He was but one example of many in the present great move of God in Iran since the revolution.

When the Holy Spirit moves in power in the way of revival, the advance of the kingdom is explosive. And God can and will move on a global scale just as he has in countries such as Iran or in regions such as the Global South, which is growing from having only 18% of the Christians in the world in 1900 to having an estimated 77% by 2050.[82]

By all means, let's pray for and wait for the extraordinary work of the Spirit in revival and reformation. In the meantime, we press on in doing the ordinary work—evangelism, discipleship, and church planting also in the power of the Holy Spirit.

CASE STUDY:
SARAH AND SOLOMON, MIDDLE EASTERN TENTMAKER PASTORS

Sarah and Solomon are a husband-and-wife team who lead a church in the Middle East. They are "tentmakers," or self-supporting workers serving in a region that has experienced great turmoil in recent years. At the same time, they have seen a powerful move of the Holy Spirit that is sweeping many from the unreached population into God's kingdom.

SOLOMON

How did you come to faith in Christ?

When I was twenty-one years old, I came to Christ. I was attending the church where we now are from a young age. My mother came to faith out of the Muslim religion at age thirteen. Up until I was twenty-one, I knew Jesus, and I was going to church, but I was living a double life. But when I was twenty-one years old, I heard a sermon. And it was like the sermon was about me and the life that I was living. After that sermon, everything started to change in my life. It really touched my heart because the preacher had the same sins. This pastor told how he came to Jesus and found redemption and forgiveness for his sins. I knew this was for me. It was God speaking to me.

Earlier I had prayed, "If you're really there, please show yourself to me, Lord." And I had gone to church with that question, with that longing. And when I was sitting there and heard this sermon, I knew God was speaking to me.

How did you become a businessman?

For a long time, I worked in several businesses—for about 20 years. From a young age, I was making auto parts. I worked somewhere for a long time, and they really did me wrong because I was working there like it was my own place. But I was praying to God: "Please provide another job" because I was working so hard, but I didn't get a really good pay. And because of their wrongdoing, I was fired. I was suddenly on my own.

When I got fired, they didn't give me anything. There was no severance pay. And it was really hard. I didn't have any money because, yes, we were newly wed and I had to tell my wife. It was a really big shock. Our first child was just 3 months old.

But God showed me through his word that he would help us. "Don't be afraid. I am with you." And for nine months, I had no work. I had no income, no work. And we were praying together. In our culture, when you get married, they give you gold things. So, we had that. When we were praying, Sarah said to me, "We have that gold. Let's sell the gold, and let's start our own business. It might be small, but God will bless it. We will start really small."

At first I said, no we can't do that. We are not going to do it. And Sarah said to me, we have nothing to lose. Let's trust in God and let's take this step with him together. And then we started our business small. We opened a small place. And with everything that we had, we bought all that was needed for the business.

And when we opened this business, we prayed, may this workplace be a workplace that serves God. After that, for five years, we were really starting the new business. We had to learn new things, and of course, God was blessing it. But we didn't see, really, that it was serving God. Of course, we were serving in church and all those things, but we didn't see exactly how it served God. But we saw that God really blessed our workplace. Praise God. What the church needed or what had to be bought, we were able to buy.

The pastor at the church then got a paycheck every month. We praise God—we could help with that through our business. And we started praying to have workers that are Christians in our workplace. And then the disaster happened. And now we have Christian workers, praise God. Two workers came to Christ after the disaster, women who are working there. It's mainly women and just one man.

Sometimes I invite them all so they don't have to work, and they're at the women's gathering in church, and we're singing worship songs together and it's so great. So, the two who were baptized also work at our workplace, praise God. One is starting to read the Bible, and yes, it's great.

What motivates you in conducting your business?

I believe that God gave me this workplace to support our church. And he said that this is what we prayed for. You need to be careful for what you pray for! It's great. We are supporting the church, but also outside of the church. Of course, you know that we are serving God outside of the church and the villages and everywhere. I am the pastor of the church, but we don't want any money from the church. We want to give; we don't want to take money from the church because right now, our church grew after the disaster. Praise God. It's so, so good. The Holy Spirit is working. It's amazing, yes, but it's really clear to us. Yes. Don't take money from the church. Give money to the church because there's a bigger blessing. It's such a great blessing because God provides everything!

The people that are coming are poor. They lost everything, but they found Jesus, praise God, the most important thing. They don't have money to help the church. So, how else do we use our workplace? Someone says, "I need work." We say, "Come to our workplace." What was that saying? Teach a man how to fish and he will have all the fish he needs. So, we're teaching people how to fish.

Yes, because our workplace is helping people, we can give and share. They see the love of God in that. Yes, I can't explain it to you. It's like I'm coming there, and somebody says to me, "Can you pray with me today?" Like, it's a really different workplace. It's a blessed workplace. Yes, we have Bibles, boxes of Bibles in our workplace. And sometimes I put on a worship song.

We also have a lot of stuff at our work from people who lost their homes but didn't lose their refrigerator or their stove. If they want to store their things somewhere, they have to pay money for that. But we said, "Okay, we have a place—just store it in our workplace. And if you find a home, if you find a little house or something, then you can take your things so you don't have to pay for it."

We're happier and we have a better life than before, and that's really hard to understand. But God gives what this world cannot.

What advice would you give to other business people who want to use their business to serve the Lord?

God is always the first priority in your life and in your work.

And don't take steps without asking him. So first, ask him. At first I took steps without asking, and it didn't go well. So I learned that I have to ask God first what step to take.

And don't think that you can do it with your own strength. You really need God, yes.

SARAH

Sarah, how did you come to faith?

I think it's important to know that my father came to faith when he was, like, sixteen years old. He comes from a Muslim family and he was born and raised here in this region where I'm living now. When he came to faith, he had to flee.

So he came to live in Europe. And yes, he went to a European church. That's the church I was born and raised in. But he went on a vacation after he came to faith. He came on a vacation to the Middle East a couple of years later. And he married my mother, also from a Muslim family. But the family didn't know my father was a Christian and they said yes, it's okay. You're living in Europe. So yes, that's a big catch for us because they thought, he can send us money then, every month. And yes, that's how they think.

They said yes [to the marriage] and then my grandfather heard that his daughter married a Christian. But at that time, they were already in Europe after they got married. But he said the first bullet from my gun is for you. So, there was a big threat.

But praise God, we were raised in a European church and after years, we were welcomed here again. And yes, I was born and raised in a Christian church. And I think my whole youth, my father preached the gospel to the Muslims in Europe. So, I always felt like I didn't know who I was. I thought, Okay, I'm a Christian, but my roots are Muslim. I feel European, so I don't feel Middle Eastern. So, I really didn't know myself. So I got into a really big depression when I was twenty years old. Really big depression. And one night, I was so depressed that I cried out to God: "Who am I?" And yes, at that moment, God really touched my heart. He really touched my heart and said, "You are mine. You are chosen."

So yes. And that was the moment that I was filled with the Holy Spirit. And I was like, Okay, I'm a child of God. Jesus Christ loves me and he knows who I am. Yes, it was a moment that night I can't explain. I never felt that way before or after. Yes. And after that, I was really focused on asking, What does God want with my life? Because before that I was doing it myself. It wasn't really making me happy, so I thought, I have to do this differently. And then the Holy Spirit moved me.

And I came on a vacation here to the Middle East. Solomon saw me in church. He was playing worship songs on his guitar. And Solomon said, "This is the girl I want to marry." And within two weeks, I was engaged. And in one year's time, I was married. But my whole family in Europe were like, Are you crazy? What are you doing? You're on vacation. How did you get engaged in two weeks' time? My father and mother were also with me, of course, when I was here on a vacation. But it was really clear that God said to me, I have a plan here for you. And I want you here. And that's where it all started.

So how do you use your role as Solomon's partner and homemaker to serve the Lord in his mission?

That's the beauty of marriage. God uses both of you to do his will. Solomon can't do this on his own and I can't do this on my own. We really need each other to grow in Christ and to learn from him together. Also, we found out that we have to stay really close to God because we're really busy. We're partners, we're really partners, in the business, at church, and at home. We're doing this together.

Just like in the Body of Christ, the hand can't say to the feet, "I don't need you." It's also like when you're married. We need each other.

Yes, because this is our life. God put me here to do his work, to serve him. That's the only reason I'm here. Yes, this is my calling. Is it easy? No, it's not an easy calling. But is it a fulfilling calling? It's really fulfilling. And it's amazing. But is it easy? No. Like, we have struggles. The darkness is not sitting still. One woman who got baptized this

Sunday—her whole family, the day after, said, "We don't want to talk to you anymore." And so we praise God that we have a new sister in Christ. And that we are a family. But if you look at her blood relatives, they don't want to talk to her. What can we do? We support her. We're praying with her. We're guiding her, going to her, calling her every day. So it's really busy, working for God. It's a busy job, and yes, it's a battle. But, praise God, he also provides a solution.

Do you want to add anything more to how you use your vocation and for the mission?

As I said, we have a lot of Bibles stored at the shop. It's a storage place for Christ. All the stuff that we have there. If something comes in that we have to deliver to the people and share the message of the gospel, it first comes into our workplace. And we store it there. From there we put it in the van and go to the villages. The Bibles, as we said, for people, and free storage for their stuff. Those who lost everything and have some things they want to store for free can do so. This allows us to share God's love and yes, his open heart. It gives us many ways for sharing. You have people that have so many needs. Yes, people who need work. The door is open. Yes, and for the support of the church.

What advice might you give to other people who want to be engaged in the mission?

I had this conversation with a girl who is a Christian. And she has a voice which is so beautiful. And she said to me, I don't know how God wants to use me.

And you know that my husband is the pastor, so he preaches in church. But also, there was another pastor. He's not at our church anymore. He left the church. There's an awakening happening, and a lot of people come. And so you have to be really open-minded and really show God's love. You don't judge immediately. You don't make people do things. No, just come. Be free. Let's praise together. Let's read the Bible together, yes.

But [this pastor] was a bit rigid and caught up in rules—we have to do this and we can't do that. We can't baptize these people. I believe we let them come to Christ, and then they will change. And then they can take the Lord's Supper.

But he felt they couldn't do that because they were not long enough in church. But the Bible says how we are to take the bread and the wine, and how you can get baptized. It's simple. You say yes, I believe in you, Jesus Christ. I want to give my life to you. And that's it. I'm laying my old life down. And it's not that complicated, but [this pastor] was really against it.

And then we said, as a church, it's really hard to work with you like this. We think in this new time of revival, you'll have to change. But he couldn't change. So, God sent him somewhere else. And so, Solomon is now leading worship. And after that, he's preaching. And so, this girl said to me, "I don't know what to do. I don't know if God wants me to come to your church and to do the praise and worship there." And I said to her, "God has given you a talent; come and use it. You just use it. That's it. Yes, God gives it to you to use."

God blesses you. Share it, use it, and give it away. Because I found out after the disaster, I didn't know what to do. But God leads you everywhere. Everywhere you go, he just wants you to share. He wants you to share the blessing, share the gospel. He wants you to give love and compassion to people. He wants you to have an open heart to other people. Open your doors and God leads everything by the Holy Spirit. You don't have to do anything and you don't have to question yourself. God gives the strength to do it. God gives the power to do it. God open doors to do it. And the Holy Spirit is working. Be encouraged.

This is how it was meant to be. Like the awakening that is happening here, that never happened before. It never happened before.

Questions for Reflection and Discussion

1. Have you ever heard or read about revivals or moves of God?

2. How did they come about?

3. What were the effects?

4. Have you ever seen or experienced a renewal or revival?

Chapter 13

Working Together as the Body of Christ

If you love me, you will keep my commandments.
—John 14:15

In July 1974, some 2,400 Christian leaders from 150 countries met in Lausanne, Switzerland, to pray and plan for world evangelization. God used Billy Graham to initiate the gathering and Ralph Winter to introduce the concept of "unreached people groups" to sharpen the focus of the remaining task for world evangelization. John Stott had the privilege of chairing the committee which drafted the landmark *Lausanne Covenant*.

Stirred by the Holy Spirit, these leaders affirmed the purposes of God:

> He has been calling out from the world a people for himself, and sending his people back into the world to be his servants and his witnesses, for the extension of his kingdom, the building up of Christ's body, and the glory of his name.

At the same time, they confessed their past failures but dedicated themselves anew to the remaining task, confident that God can and will use earthen vessels:

> We confess with shame that we have often denied our calling and failed in our mission, by becoming conformed to the world or by withdrawing from it. Yet we rejoice that, even when borne by earthen vessels, the gospel is still a precious treasure. To the task of making that treasure known in the power of the Holy Spirit we desire to dedicate ourselves anew.

They further asserted that God uses the whole Body of Christ for the sacred task:

> World evangelization requires the whole Church to take the whole gospel to the whole world. The Church is at the very centre of God's cosmic purpose and is his appointed means of spreading the gospel.

And finally, they affirmed the necessity of working together:

> We affirm that the Church's visible unity in truth is God's purpose. Evangelism also summons us to unity, because our oneness strengthens our witness, just as our disunity undermines our gospel of reconciliation. . . . We urge the development of regional and functional cooperation for the furtherance of the Church's mission, for strategic planning, for mutual encouragement, and for the sharing of resources and experience.[83]

Oral Roberts University Professor of Global Christianity Wonsuk Ma asserts the article of faith about working as the whole Body must be realized in practice. In a 2023 article he points out "the biggest challenge is that only tiny fractions of today's church are directly involved in mission."[84]

He calls for a shift from relying only on the "elitist" mission models of the past, which tend to relegate the mission to professionals only, to also including the equally biblical democratized paradigm described in Acts 11, which is not dependent on Western resources.[85] This shift will be especially appropriate as the vast majority of all Christians will live in the Global South by 2050.[86]

Dr. Ma goes on to cite the example of the Bhojpuri Breakthrough in northeast India, which had once been known as the "graveyard of missionaries," with only .0001% Christians in the Hindu heartland of one hundred million. But within three decades, there were twelve million believers as the result of a move of the Spirit among national leaders using a holistic approach with local resources.

Questions for Reflection and Discussion

1. Dr. Ma stated, "The biggest challenge is that only tiny fractions of today's church are directly involved in mission." How can this issue be addressed?

2. A great shift in the global church has been taking place from Europe and North America to the "Global South," i.e., countries in Africa, Latin America, Asia, and the Pacific. How might this affect our mission involvement?

Chapter 14

Your Identity as a Witness

We need to recover the truth that every Christian is a missionary.
—Dr. J. Christy Wilson

Amar Peterman struggled with the problem of disability until the Lord gave him light on the matter. He tells his story of finding his identity as a witness in *Sojourners* online magazine:

> For most of my life, the reality of disability and the problem of evil were one in the same. I constantly found myself asking the same question:
>
> Why did God let this happen to me?
>
> For me, "this" referred to contracting polio as an orphan in India, leading to irreparable damage in my right leg. Others might ask a similar question due to a lack of norepinephrine and dopamine in their brain or an injury from a car accident caused by a drunk driver. In some cases, God is the sole object of our frustration. In other circumstances, a human individual is at fault.

My inability to answer this question for most of my life led to a deep resentment toward God. The times when I got maddest at God did not warrant the wrath I allowed them to create, like when I was picked last for a pickup game of kickball or couldn't fit into a trendy pair of Vans or had an oversized leg brace poking through my skinny jeans. These things certainly did not warrant the wrath I allowed them to create. But, at the time, those were meaningful things to me. As a dark kid in a sea of whiteness, these were missed opportunities to blend in with my peers rather than be labeled as an outcast. . . .

Time after time, these Christians would lay hands on me while I waited in line at Starbucks or the food court at the local mall. They'd try and cast out evil demons, pray that my faith would be strengthened, or command in Jesus' name that I get up and walk (even though I could already walk). Each time, they would stand back as if they'd just recited the magic words. Each time, with progressively less optimism and greater anger, I'd step forward only to find out I wasn't healed. Some would accuse me of not having enough faith, but most just apologized and went on with their day. I was left alone. Still limping, still furious. . . . "Why does an all-powerful God allow bad things to happen to good people" became deeply personal: "Why is an all-powerful God allowing this to happen to me?"

In John 9:2–3, the disciples encounter a man who has been blind since birth and they ask Jesus a similar question: "Who sinned, this man or his parents, that he was born blind?" Jesus replies, "Neither this man nor his parents sinned; he was born blind *so that God's works might be revealed in him*" (emphasis added).

In this passage, Jesus rearticulates the problem of pain and God's sovereignty. Rather than affirming that it is sin that causes disability, Jesus centers on the purposes of God. . . . But to summarize theologian Shelly Rambo's reflection on finding meaning in suffering, the God who calls us to this task is one whose resurrected body bears crucifixion wounds. Even more, the resurrected wounds of Jesus become a means for others to "feel their way into the world again." Jesus' wounds are not a hindrance to gospel proclamation, they are a gospel proclamation.[87]

As we have seen, **a root of the problem of rising numbers of unreached is that mission engagement is not part of the identity of most Christians.** *The truth that every Christian is a missionary must be recovered.*

As we recover this truth, the sleeping giant will rise up to receive God's call, and the number of unreached will start its inevitable downward trajectory. People of every tribe and in every condition have this call. As mentioned, the recovery of this essential truth will require a mighty move of God the Holy Spirit; a spiritual problem requires a spiritual solution. It will not come about through programs, plans, promotions, campaigns, or any other merely human means. As God's people come together and ask him, we will be halfway towards seeing the problem solved. The opposition of the devil, the world, and the flesh will be swept aside and subdued as we pray.

As mentioned, in the spiritual realm, progress often comes through the process of **recovery**, just as in the secular world progress comes through the process of **discovery**. The modern technological revolution came about as people discovered how to miniaturize electronic components and how to apply the lessons of mathematics and symbolic logic to create ever more intelligent applications to run on them.

Great advances of the Kingdom of God occurred after Martin Luther and the other Reformers *recovered* the gospel. More great advances came after William Carey helped to *recover* the Great

Commission for the Protestant Church. Similarly, great advances in world evangelization will follow recovering the truth that every Christian is a missionary.

As Richard Lovelace has shown, orientation to mission is a part of the fruit of renewal. As we pray for revival and see God answer, there will be a resurgence of interest and engagement in the mission. He writes:

> One cannot help but wonder what the result would be if this mass of lay people could be spiritually released from their servitude in the American success system and reoriented to channel their major energies toward building the kingdom of God. Foreign mission would be enriched with a new flow of personnel and resources—contrary to some perceptions of the situation there is still room for this—and on the home missionary front there would be not only a surge of evangelism-in-depth comparable to the awakenings on the mission field but also the provision of funds needed for a whole variety of ministries from social compassion to the media.[88]

QUESTIONS FOR REFLECTION AND DISCUSSION

1. Mission engagement is not part of the identity of most Christians. Do you agree or disagree with this statement?

2. If mission engagement is not part of the modern Christian identity, how can this be effectively addressed?

CHAPTER 15

FOR EVERY FOLLOWER OF CHRIST: YOUR VOCATION AS A MINISTRY

> *Whatever you do, work heartily, as for the Lord and not for men, knowing that from the Lord you will receive the inheritance as your reward. You are serving the Lord Christ.*
> —COLOSSIANS 3:23–24

WHEN I WORKED COUNSELING with people who had been in trouble with the law, I quickly realized that the root problem was spiritual, and, therefore all the therapy, punishment, psychology, and "treatment" in the world would be powerless to really transform them. So I shared the gospel that saved my life if they granted me permission to share with them from one person to another, above and beyond the official role I had. When they really took in the gospel, it was transformative, and committing crimes stopped being an option.

Whatever your vocation is, you are doing it for the Lord, if you are a Christian. Knowing Christ transforms any vocation from merely being a job into a ministry. The work we do takes on a new meaning that transforms it and gives it eternal value because our work in the Lord is never in vain (1 Corinthians 15:58).

As we have seen, vocations are callings from God; work is not drudgery done merely for a paycheck. God gives us vocations that we might use them to glorify him, serve others, and advance his kingdom. Every vocation can become a ministry if it is done for Christ.

As we move forward in the twenty-first century, a number of megatrends set the stage for a new phase in global missions. The rise of AI and the hyper-connected world implies further harnessing social media and other communications technology to make the gospel freely available throughout the world. Partial deglobalization, political fragmentation, and geopolitical conflict mean the traditional Western-supported "elitist" models of the past will not always be practical ways of reaching the unreached. This is an opportune time for the more democratized approach of the "John 17" way. A wider use of indigenous tentmakers, along with a greater harnessing of emerging technologies, enable the Church to overcome these emerging obstacles to conventional missions.

The case studies in this book feature stories of Christians who are using their vocations to serve the Lord in his mission. Businessmen, a homemaker, a doctor, a retiree, a translator, and others share how they are serving the Lord in his mission using their vocations. These inspiring "tentmakers" come from around the world, including the US, the Middle East, South America, Africa, and Asia.

The Apostle Paul and his remarkable ministry provide the template not only for the special call but also for the general call to carry out the mission. He has given career missionaries a clear model of what it means to be cross-cultural missionaries by planting the Church cross-culturally throughout the ancient world.

But he has also given a clear model for what it means for the ordinary Christian to follow Christ into the mission of God. Paul was a tentmaker, and often supported himself by making tents, even though at other times he accepted financial support from others in the church (Philippians 4:15–18).

He supported himself when possible in order to freely offer the gospel, which is freely given:

> Who serves as a soldier at his own expense? Who plants a vineyard and does not eat its grapes? Who tends a flock and does not drink the milk? . . . If we have sown spiritual seed among you, is it too much if we reap a material harvest from you? If others have this right of support from you, shouldn't we have it all the more?
>
> But we did not use this right. On the contrary, we put up with anything rather than hinder the gospel of Christ. Don't you know that those who serve in the temple get their food from the temple, and that those who serve at the altar share in what is offered on the altar? In the same way, the Lord has commanded that those who preach the gospel should receive their living from the gospel.
>
> But I have not used any of these rights. . . . What then is my reward? Just this: that in preaching the gospel I may offer it free of charge, and so not make full use of my rights as a preacher of the gospel (I Corinthians 9:7–18).

When you serve the Lord in his mission as a self-supporting worker, you are demonstrating the gospel you proclaim. You are freely giving the gospel which has been given freely. You are bearing the cost yourself, and, in this way, imitating the one who sent you. You are part of a vast army of disciples who are being used by God to extend his Kingdom.

Case Study: Mariana, South American Physical Therapist and Tentmaker

Mariana is a physical therapist and a pastor's wife. She lives and works in South America. As a dedicated Christian, she uses her vocation as a physical therapist to serve the Lord and to provide her patients help beyond physical therapy and rehabilitation.

How did you become a Christian?

My parents are pastors. I received the Lord when I was eight years old. But it was not until I was twenty-five years old that I really committed myself to serving the Lord.

How did you come to take up your present vocation?

I'm a physical therapist and kinesiologist. I studied physical therapy at university and immediately started working in a hospital. Then I started a private practice. I've also taken quite a number of courses and postgraduate courses as well.

What motivates you to do your work?

I'm married to a pastor and the mother of two children. It's partly in order to provide for my family and to find professional fulfillment as well. For me, it's a tremendous thing when I see that my profession can help and bless other people.

How do you use your vocation to serve the Lord?

Years ago, I wanted to study medicine in the public university here, thinking it would be a good way to make quite a bit of money. But when I decided to commit myself to the Lord, my perspective changed a lot.

And so when I became a physical therapist and started to practice this and have patients come in, as they walk in the door, they hear Christian music. I try to give them an atmosphere that lets them know that I'm a believer. That's an atmosphere that I want to create, beginning when the patients first come in.

My profession involves one-on-one relationships and I spend a significant amount of time with each patient who receives treatment with me. I'll spend at least forty minutes per patient in an appointment and I'll have significant time to spend time with them and speak to them as well.

What advice would you give to another Christian who's going into a healthcare profession?

When it comes to health issues, when people are sick or need treatment, they seem to be more open to sharing with you. They don't put up resistance to pretty deep conversations.

As they're seeking health or relief from pain, I have had the opportunity to listen to quite a number of testimonies of people I have worked with, both good and bad.

And I take advantage of that, because I see that opportunity to share with them that there is a God who can heal them. He doesn't always do so. He sometimes uses other means, like physical therapy. And I have real experience with him and I can share that experience with them as well.

They often perceive that I'm a a Christian, or that I believe in God. And they will ask me questions about that and I can share with them that yes, I'm a believer. I'm an evangelical believer and I'd like to share with them what God has done for me and people are very open to that. And very rarely will they reject that and I have had opportunities to ask them if I can I pray for them about their situation. They almost always will say yes I would like that. I would really like that. That starts a relationship, and I can invite them or even challenge them to perhaps get involved in a church or come to know God.

I would like everyone, every believer who works in the health professions, to understand that. Life is unsure. Life is short. You never know when someone may only be there with you for the last time, and to take advantage of that time to challenge them to seek God and to come to know him. You never know if that's going to be your last opportunity.

Right now, my husband is a pastor of a church here in the city. My husband and I have taken many courses. I see the importance not only of training for my career as a physical therapist, but also to continue to challenge and prepare ourselves to minister to other people, to learn how to share the word of God better. I'm involved in trauma healing courses, to help needy people work through grief or other issues that have caused trauma. And we see the need to not let one day go by where we haven't shared with at least one person that God loves them. God wants them to know him and live a life pleasing to him. So, I've had many opportunities in the church as well as outside to continue to grow and to become better trained to share the love of Jesus with others in secular as well as church settings.

I'm also in charge of the Ladies' Ministry in the church, teaching the Bible in that context. I work on Saturday, teaching a group of children. It's called Mission Adventures, and we try to train and challenge children to get involved in missions and consider missions in their future.

So do you have any words of advice for other women who are working in the church, perhaps in the role of a pastor's wife?

I understand very well, just like the other mothers and wives who are in the church, how hard it is to manage the work-life balance. And how hard and challenging it is to be a mother, taking care of children, handling a profession, and serving in the church. But take advantage of every opportunity. If you have a real conviction, a calling from God, he will provide opportunities to take advantage of, whether big or small.

Make the most of the time you have. It is vital to see how God is working and to cooperate with him. You know, despite time limitations and other challenges, serve him and use your time well and then leave things in his hands. When I was younger, I served on the puppet and drama team. I was very active in that, along with my sister and mother. My mother makes the puppets.

In one case, a widow lost her husband during the pandemic. He was a pastor. She lives here in the city. I worked with some widows, and she came on a retreat we had. She is from a humble background, but she was encouraged by the fellowship with the other widows. But a few months later, she was hit and run over by a car.

I saw her again and she was very depressed. She lost a good bit of her hand, a whole section of her hand. She just has a thumb and a little finger left. At first, she didn't want to go on living. "It would have been better if I had just died in this accident," she said. "First I lost my husband and now this happened." She was very depressed. It would have been better to have died, she said. I became her psychologist as well as her physical therapist.

Another person who had a terrible accident lost his leg. These two individuals were coming at the same time. He, too, was also extremely discouraged and depressed. Both of these individuals are believers. The daughter of the man who was injured is on the puppet team. When she saw what happened to her father, it was very traumatic for her. She was angry at God.

To her mother, she admitted that she has never come to know the Lord as her Savior, but now she has come to know the Lord as her Savior. With me, in this same room about a month ago, she realized what God did in her father's life, as well as some of the things that we learned in our studies together about what salvation really is. She made the decision to come to Christ and saw all those things work together for good in the end.

One doctor told this young man: You'll never be able to walk again. But then he started coming to me about four or five months ago. And I've been working with this lady who had the accident, the widow, as well as this young man. These are two situations that are fairly recent that I've been working with, not just physically. And we are seeing tremendous strides and encouragement.

So both of them have realized that there was a reason the accident happened to them. They have learned lessons from it, and God had a good purpose even through these tragedies. They are recovering much of their ability and are overcoming their disabilities.

In the case of the widow, shortly after this accident happened, she stopped going to church and was just very depressed. But now, you know, I've seen a real transformation in her. Now she's gone back to church and she's very involved in a lot of different ministries there. She even goes to funerals. Despite having lost her husband, she's able to be used by God powerfully in those ministries as well. Her attitude has been transformed. She has been able to accept what happened to her. And I've seen she has less embarrassment about people seeing her hand.

She thought she'd have to stop her work making ice cream. But she's been able to go back to making ice cream. She's gone back to that. It's just very encouraging. And the young man has also started driving again. He's a bus driver. He has been able to get back to that even with his leg injury. I have seen a real turnaround in their cases.

Questions for Reflection and Discussion

1. What is your vocation or calling in life? How can you be a blessing and a witness for Christ as you do your work?

2. As missions in the 21st century moves to more "democratic" models, what part will "tentmakers" play?

CHAPTER 16

FOR CHRISTIAN LEADERS: YOUR CRUCIAL ROLE

> And he gave the apostles, the prophets,
> the evangelists, the shepherds and teachers, to
> equip the saints for the work of ministry,
> for building up the body of Christ.
> —EPHESIANS 4:11–12

> Now that you know these things,
> you will be blessed if you do them.
> —JOHN 13:17 NIV

BILLY GRAHAM ONCE OBSERVED, "J. Christy Wilson will go down in history as one of the great and courageous missionaries for the gospel in the twentieth century."

When Christy was at Princeton, he was the captain of the track team. One of the traditions was a one-mile relay race, and Christy was the anchor for his team. A wealthy alumnus donated gold medals each year for the winners. In a competing class team, Dana "Skip" Payne was running and Christy knew Skip was faster than he was.

During the race, the first three runners gained a slight lead for Christy, the anchor. He received the baton a few feet ahead of Skip and ran as fast as he could, but he could hear Skip gaining ground. But Skip ran too close to him and Christy's hand unwittingly hit his baton and knocked it to the ground. By the time Skip picked it up, Christy had already won the race.

Christy felt terrible about the accident, and that night he went to Skip's dorm and offered him the gold medal, but he refused to take it. Christy went on to tell him of a far greater prize that Jesus Christ had won for him. They talked far into the night, and Skip ended up receiving Jesus as his Savior.

Christy Wilson went on to become the modern pioneer missionary to Afghanistan. There were no known Christians when he and his wife Betty went there in 1951, but by the time he left, the number was probably in the low thousands. After a death threat against him, he and his wife returned to America in 1973. A prophetic word was given that said he would be used even more after he returned to the US than when he was on the field. He went on to teach and inspire a generation of missionaries and seminary students at Gordon-Conwell Seminary for seventeen years.

Although I am not a pastor, I want to share my experience as a fellow elder in the hope it will prove helpful and encouraging to pastors and other church leaders who have the high calling of leading God's people. My experience fits perfectly with what I read in the Lord's Last Discourse.

When my wife and I first attended the church where we worship, I noticed two families had disabled teenage children they brought to church with them. It wasn't clear if these poor children could understand anything that was being said. But what was clear was that they were loved by the parents, the other believers, and the church leaders. This impressed me because you don't always see this.

I have had the privilege of being a part of two local churches that have had something of the John 17 mission dynamic. In each case, the senior pastors were faithful to really love their flocks and preach the gospel of the extravagant love of God freely and graciously given. Simply expounding the gospel and other biblical truth alone is not enough to bring about transformation. In each case, the pastor's love of the flock confirmed the truth of the gospel he preached (1 Cor. 13:1). Other means of grace are needed as well. These include vivid representations of the gospel, such as the celebration of communion. These demonstrations of the gospel bring the message home powerfully.

Just as the Last Discourse sets out, knowing Christ and following his command to love one another as he loves us forms the foundation for the work of the church. This was certainly true under the leadership of Dr. Halverson at Fourth Presbyterian Church, as each member carried the vision of being Christ's witnesses between Sundays wherever Christ took us.

Every Sunday at Fourth Presbyterian Church, he famously pronounced this benediction:

> You go nowhere by accident. Wherever you go, God is sending you there. Wherever you are, God has put you

there. He has a purpose in your being there. Christ, who indwells you, has something He wants to do through you, wherever you are. Believe this, and go in His grace and love and power.

During the time I worshipped at Fourth, I took these words to heart. I saw my counseling work as being a witness for Christ and encouraging those I worked with in their own faith journeys. I recognized my calling was beyond the humanistic rehabilitation system I worked in, and for that reason I sometimes took on the role of a chaplain. This benediction had great power because it came from the heart of God and derived from the truth that every Christian is a missionary. As the Father sent our Savior, so the Savior sends you and me into the world. This benediction was a distinctive way of casting Christ's vision for how his Church is to be carrying the work forward, and it has affected me to this day.

At the church where my wife and I now worship, both the present senior pastor and his predecessor set the stage for the church members to flourish in their gifting and callings by faithfully proclaiming the gospel of grace and demonstrating it through their love for Christ's Church. This foundational work created a context where I personally have felt the freedom and encouragement to pursue my calling without hindrance. And I'm not an isolated case. I see others who are also able to thrive in the ministries of music, worship, and in pursuing local outreach ministries such as an ESL program for the community.

So much rises and falls on leadership. God has called pastors and other church leaders to the high privilege of leading his beloved Church, which he bought with his own blood. We will all stand before the righteous judge to give an account of the deeds done in the flesh

(2 Corinthians 5:9). Of course, there will be no condemnation for those who are in Christ, but rather he will reward each one for his or her works. For Christian leaders, the standard will be higher because leaders have greater access to the knowledge of the things of God and a higher level of grace and gifting for ministry.

Christian leaders will also be accountable not only for their own work but also for the work of the saints entrusted to their care. Just as the coach of the champion team shares in the victory of his team, the pastors and other leaders will be rewarded not only for their own work but also for the fruitful work of their congregations and charges.

Christian leaders in general and pastors in particular, therefore, have a golden opportunity to lead their churches in recovering mission engagement as part of their identity as Christians. All leadership is by example. If the senior pastor really loves the flock, the church members will love one another. If he proclaims and lives out the gospel of grace, his church will more freely enjoy and share this amazing gospel. And if the senior pastor is deeply engaged in the mission, his congregants will follow suit.

Pastors, denominational leaders and other Christian leaders are also well positioned to enter into coalitions and partnerships to advance the gospel in the John 17 way. The Gospel Coalition, Urbana (the annual InterVarsity student missions conference), SAT-7 (the media ministry for the Middle East), PAK7 (the media ministry for Pakistan), and the Lausanne Movement are all examples of organizations that local churches and denominations can connect with to advance the mission together.

The John 17 vision begins with the command of Christ to love one another as he loves us—freely, fully, and forever. The John 17 Way begins with the love of Christ, leads to greater works, and ends with the world being able to see Christ and hear the gospel.

There are no ten easy steps to making your church mission-minded. The process of fruitfulness is organic and spiritual. But if the pastor is all in for Christ and the advance of the gospel and loves the flock with the love of God, a fire will be kindled. And that fire can spread to the ends of the earth.

Questions for Reflection and Discussion

1. Why does so much rise and fall with leadership?

2. Why is the love command in the Last Discourse foundational for Jesus' vision for his mission as laid out in the Last Discourse?

3. Can you think of examples of church members who have been encouraged by their leaders to discover and use their gifts as they find their place in the Lord's family?

Chapter 17

The Real "Mission From God" Appeal

> We should not underestimate the significance of
> the small group of people who have a vision of a
> just and gentle world. The quality of a whole culture
> may be changed when two percent of
> its people have a new vision.
>
> —Robert Bellah

Steve Jobs always had a passion to "put a dent in the world." In 1982, as Apple began to see a surge in its growth due to the success of the Apple II series computers, Steve Jobs realized, at age twenty-eight, he was not yet qualified to run a large company. He needed to recruit a talented, seasoned CEO. John Sculley, the CEO of Pepsi, fit the bill. Pepsi's earnings and stock price were rising rapidly as a result of Sculley's successful marketing campaigns.

Jobs set out to court Sculley, and the two became friends in late 1982. Jobs saw him and courted him just about every weekend through

March of 1983. In spite of Steve's efforts, Sculley finally told him, "Steve, I've thought about it, and I'm not coming to Apple."

Steve paused and looked straight into Sculley's eyes before famously making the irresistible appeal: "Do you want to sell sugar water for the rest of your life, or do you want to come with me and change the world?" Sculley joined Apple the next month, and Apple continued on its trajectory to become the largest company in the world.[89] This kind of appeal to come and change the world became known in the business world as "the mission from God" appeal.

If I were to try to recruit the CEO of Apple or some other large corporation to become part of the mission of God, I might well make a similar appeal: "Do you want to sell gadgets for the rest of your life, or do you want to come with us and really transform the world?"

No one can deny that the iPhone has put a dent in the world. The digital revolution has dramatically changed how we live. Yet at the same time, mere temporal transformations are castles in the sand, which the tide of eternity will one day wash away. But the transformation that Jesus Christ brings is profound, infinite, and eternal. He alone is able to change the heart and so deeply transform the lives of people in all nations. So, if you really want to change the world in the most significant possible way, come and become part of the mission of God! Why settle for a merely metaphorical mission from God when you can be part of the real thing?

I might add that following Christ and becoming part of his mission doesn't need to mean quitting your secular job. For some, it may mean leaving the corporate world to go on the mission field, but for most others, it might well mean being a CEO for Christ, staying in the vocation God has called you to but doing the work for Christ's glory and to extend his kingdom, and not just to earn a living and advance your career.

Jimmy Carter was a great example of someone who understood he was in this world to serve a higher purpose. He knew he was here for more than just peanuts and politics; he was a man with a mission. He glorified the Savior he loved by securing peace between Egypt and Israel, helping to eradicate Guinea worm disease, building homes for the poor, championing racial reconciliation, teaching Sunday School, and loving his neighbor. He "walked humbly with his God."

Case Study: John, American CEO and Tentmaker

John is the sole proprietor and CEO of a successful business. He is devoted to the Lord and has the gift of radical generosity. He joyfully gives away much, if not most, of the considerable wealth his business generates, supporting a variety of missions and ministries in a very significant way. He serves on the missions team of his local church and has a ministry of personal witness and providing inspirational Christian books.

How did you come to faith?

I remember it well. At the Mennonite Church, around age ten, there was a minister who held revival meetings. I came to faith in Christ through them.

How did you become a businessman?

My father was a barn painter, a businessman. But I never wanted to paint barns. I remember in third grade I loved math and numbers. I was also taken by a story about a boy who raised guppies and I started to dream about getting my own aquarium. I read as many books as I could find on fish, and for three years I saved and bought one, then two aquariums. I started raising guppies.

At sixteen, my dad found an ad for a tropical fish store for sale for $3,500. He said to call them and maybe we could get a good deal on the aquarium and all the supplies. Dad said, "If God gives you a vision, that's better than other people's ideas." A week later we took out a loan to buy the store. I loved it. It was my dream job, buying and selling tropical fish and supplies. I was even buying tropical fish from Florida. They were packed in boxes and flown to the Lancaster Airport. I would drive out to pick up the boxes at the runway after school on my way to the store.

I moved to Washington, DC, at eighteen, after selling my store, and worked with the Agape Coffeehouse and Bookstore outreach and Young Life as a leader at Einstein High School. During that time, I met a businessman connected with Agape who suggested we start a wholesale picture-framing supply company. Now I had a chance to again work with numbers and dream about the possibilities in 1970.

What motivates you to do your work?

As Randy Alcorn outlines in *Giving is the Good Life: The Unexpected Path to Purpose and Joy*, as Christians we have three wonderful treasures.

Jesus is our first and principal eternal treasure. All else pales in comparison to him (Phil. 3:7–11). Heaven is our second treasure—a place where Christ lives and where we are to set our minds (Col. 3:1–2). Eternal rewards comprise our third treasure (Luke 16:9). Cheerfulness sometimes precedes and sometimes follows giving. When we start obeying Jesus and giving our treasure, our time, and our money, our hearts will follow with peace and joy. Giving has a redemptive quality for the giver.

So how do you use your vocation and serving the Lord?

As I think about my journey through life, it is surprising how much joy I have found in giving. Generosity is a gateway to getting to know God better. And that's the thing—we were made in his image and we get to know him better by giving.

Hebrews 12:2 says, "For the joy set before him he endured the cross." Joy and giving go together. The most joyful person in heaven could be Jesus as he gets to meet all those he has redeemed by giving his life.

It even brings joy every day as I help staff and customers as they ask questions. Daily we are looking to supply their picture-framing supply needs and there are always challenges. The more we give, the more we find the joy God wants us to find.

Radical generosity and giving may fulfill our desire for financial gain. It is possible to earn more so we have more to give away. In this way, we are always learning to share our blessings with others.

Matthew 6:24 says, "No one can serve two masters—God and money." We may use our money to serve God as we seek to grow the number of people we know who are seeking to learn more about our heavenly Father.

So now in 2024, I still dream about new ways to serve my customers from Maryland to California. We serve over eight hundred customers from our various locations. It gives me a lot of connections with my customers, as well as staff, and the chance to share my dream about an amazing place we call heaven.

Questions for Reflection and Discussion

1. Has God spoken to you through anything you have read?

2. Write down how God has spoken to you.

3. How will you realize and put into practice what God has shown you?

Appendices

These appendices are useful resources to learn about and engage in missions.

This Bible Outline shows the Bible has one single theme: God's redemptive mission.

Appendix A
Bible Outline

Theme: In love, God redeems a people for himself from every tribe and nation in, through, and for the Lord Jesus Christ for his glory. The Holy Spirit applies that redemption through the Church as she obeys the Great Commission.

1. The Need for Redemption: Genesis 1–11

God created man in his own image, but man fell from his created perfection into corruption, and through Adam and Eve sin infected the entire human race.

2. The Preparation for Redemption: Genesis 12–Malachi

a. The Election of the Chosen People: 5 Books of Law

God chooses one man, Abram, through whom comes Israel, out of which will come the Messiah. God gives both the moral and ceremonial law. The moral law sets the stage for the Savior by teaching us we are sinners who need a Savior. The ceremonial law prepares the way by establishing the principle that there is no forgiveness except by shedding the blood of a substitute sacrifice.

b. The Establishment of the Chosen People: 12 Books of History

God establishes Abraham and his descendants as his people through a series of covenants. The Old is provisional, temporary, and with one ethnic people. But in it is promised a New Covenant which is final, eternal, and for people from every tribe, nation, and tongue. The books of history begin with the conquest of Canaan and tell of the fall of the divided Kingdom to Assyria and Babylon and conclude with the restoration of Judah in the sixth century BC. The books of history recount the cycles of testing, sin, judgment, repentance, and grace. These accounts of God's faithfulness and Israel's failure reveal God's holiness, righteousness, and justice as well as his love, grace, and mercy. They also clearly reveal human depravity and helplessness. Eventually, Israel's hopes for a righteous earthly king and restored kingdom were dashed, and their hope is redirected to the promised Messiah.

c. The Experience of the Chosen People: 5 Books of Wisdom and Poetry

The five books of wisdom and poetry embody Israel's inspired wisdom and worship of the God who brought them out of the bondage of paganism. They all point to Christ, "in whom are hidden all the treasures of wisdom and knowledge" (Col. 2:3).

d. The Expectation of the Chosen People: 17 Books of Prophecy

The prophets were God's spokesmen. They spoke to Israel for God not only concerning current events, but also foretold the coming Messiah of Israel and Savior of the world. Some three hundred Messianic prophecies foretell the Savior's coming into the world and his sacrificial death and resurrection to redeem a chosen people for God.

3. The Coming of Redemption: Four Gospels

The Lord Jesus Christ comes into the world, revealing his glory, conquering evil, and accomplishing our redemption through his death and resurrection.

4. The Spread of Redemption: Acts

The Holy Spirit comes upon the early church to empower the believers to preach the gospel, make disciples, and plant churches among all nations. **This book doesn't conclude.**

5. The Explanation of Redemption: 21 Epistles

The Epistles interpret, explain, and apply this great redemption.

6. The Completion of Redemption: Revelation

At the end of the Church Age, after the gospel has been proclaimed to all nations, the Lord Jesus Christ returns in great power and glory to consummate his great redemptive plan in the world, judging men and angels and reigning in majesty, for ever and ever.

Appendix B
The Heidelberg Catechism, Lord's Day 1

Tradition is not the worship of ashes,
but the preservation of fire.

—Gustav Mahler

From Heidelberg, Germany, this Catechism has been translated into many languages because it is one of the most useful teaching tools dating from the time of the Reformation. It is marked by simplicity and heartfelt devotion. It's worth memorizing.

Q. What is your only comfort in life and death?

A. That I am not my own, but belong with body and soul, both in life and in death to my faithful Savior Jesus Christ. He has fully paid for all my sins with his precious blood, and has set me free from all the power of the devil. He also preserves me in such a way that without the will of my heavenly Father not a hair can fall from my head; indeed, all things must work together for my salvation. Therefore, by his Holy Spirit he also assures me of eternal life and makes me heartily willing and ready from now on to live for him.

1 Cor 6:19, 20; Rom 14:7–9; 1 Cor 3:23; Tit 2:14; 1 Pet 1:18, 19; 1 Jn 1:7; 2:2; Jn 8:34–36; Heb 2:14, 15; 1 Jn 3:8; Jn 6:39, 40; 10:27–30; 2 Thess 3:3; 1 Pet 1:5; Mt 10:29-31; Lk 21:16–18; Rom 8:28; Rom 8:15, 16; 2 Cor 1:21, 22, 5:5; Eph 1:13, 14; Rom 8:14

Q. What do you need to know in order to live and die in the joy of this comfort?

A. First, how great my sins and misery are; second, how I am delivered from all my sins and misery; third, how I am to be thankful to God for such deliverance.

Rom 3:9,10; Jn 1:10; Jn 17:3; Acts 4:12; 10:43; Mt 5:16; Rom 6:13; Eph 5:8-10; 1 Pet 2:9, 10

Appendix C
Ten Essentials of Faith and Obedience

Whoever practices and teaches these commands will be called great in the kingdom of heaven.
—Matthew 5:19

When I worked as a counselor, I developed these Essentials as a Christian alternative or supplement to the AA Twelve Steps. They can also be used as a teaching tool in missions.

Following Jesus Christ can never be reduced to a series of steps; the Christian faith is about what Christ has done for us, not about what we do for him. The faith does not consist merely in doctrines, affections, and actions, important as these are. True Christianity is transcendent.

Nevertheless certain truths, commitments, and experiences are essential to Christian discipleship. The *Ten Essentials* is offered as a tool for pursuing discipleship and in leading others to become disciples of Jesus Christ. It can be used in individual devotions or to set the agenda for small groups. It is designed to be a "transferable concept," which can be passed on to others and so multiply disciples even where the Bible is not freely available in a particular language. In response to God's extravagant love for us in Christ and the gracious gift of eternal life, we seek to respond in kind.

1. We believed God so loved us that he gave Jesus Christ to die for our sins and to rise again from the dead so that we might have eternal life and the forgiveness of sins as gifts.

2. We confessed, turned from, and put to death anything in our lives we knew to be wrong, knowing Christ has freed us from the power and the penalty of sin through the cross.

3. We received the promised fulness of the Holy Spirit to know God better and have a fruitful life and ministry. Through him, we received the fruit, the gifts and the power of the Spirit along with Christ's authority over the powers of darkness.

4. We sought God's healing power and grace inwardly, outwardly and in our relationships with others.

5. We made a covenant to live and serve as part of the Body of Christ through active membership in a local church, putting our love for Christ above all secondary differences, celebrating God's covenant love for us through communion, and affirming our covenant love for him through baptism.

6. We loved and worshipped God wholeheartedly and exclusively in response to his great love for us, denying ourselves and taking up the cross daily to follow Christ as his disciples.

7. We joyfully loved one another as Jesus Christ has loved us and given himself for us.

8. We served Christ through regular worship, fellowship, prayer, Bible study, and witnessing for him in word and action.

9. Having received the gift of eternal life, we shared this good news with others from all nations through evangelism, discipleship, and

starting new churches, using our gifts and talents according to God's call, and passing these traditions of faith and obedience on to others.

10. Above all, we sought to do everything for the glory of God the Father, Son, and Holy Spirit.

John 3:16; Romans 6; Acts 1:8, 2:1–41; Galatians 5:22–23; Matthew 10:1; 2 Corinthians 5:17; Hebrews 10:25; Mark 14:22; 1 Corinthians 11:23–25; Mark 16:16; Matthew 22:37–40; Luke 14:26–27; John 13:34–35, 14:21–23; Matthew 6:5–15; Matthew 28:18–20; 1 Corinthians 10:3

Appendix D
A Prayer for Revival and Reformation

This is a sample prayer for revival and reformation. It is not intended to be used as a prayer to be recited, but as a starting point to stimulate the reader to formulate his or her own prayer to the Father for the advance of his kingdom.

Our Father in Heaven,

May your great name be glorified among all nations as the great Good News of your Son is made known throughout the world. May you reveal your infinite goodness—your holiness, majesty, greatness, power, righteousness, justice, grace, mercy, and love as the gospel is proclaimed and demonstrated. May your Spirit convict the world of sin and righteousness and judgment so that the gospel might be received.

Lord, please forgive our sins, which are many and serious. Not the least of them is our marginalizing and ignoring the Great Commission and repeated failure to bring the gospel to all nations as Christ commanded us so long ago. Forgive us, too, for our failure to carry out that Commission in the way Christ envisioned and commanded.

Your kingdom come. Grant to us fresh visitations of your Holy Spirit as you have promised, for it is only by His power and grace that we will be able to fulfill your mandate. And grant us the grace to ask according to your will—together in humility, brokenness, and repentance and with persistent, prevailing faith. Please do your work of convicting and converting the lost.

Fulfill the prophetic vision of Zechariah for a new global Great Awakening. And grant a new reformation to restore unity in the Body of Christ and the realization that each of us, as members of Christ's Body, has the privilege and joy of participating in your mission according to your gifting and call. Grant us grace to recover mission engagement as a normal part of following Christ. Please give us hearts after your own heart along with a passion to see the gospel preached where Christ is unknown.

We echo our Savior's Great High Priestly prayer: Make us one as you are one so the world will know you have sent him into the world to redeem us, and have loved us just as you love him.

May the gospel of your Kingdom powerfully and rapidly advance to the ends of the earth to gather in all you have called from every nation and so speed the day of your coming, Lord Jesus. Come back, Lord Jesus!

In your mighty name and for your greater glory we pray.

To connect with an ongoing online 24/7 prayer and worship meeting, visit the International House of Prayer in Kansas City, www.ihopkc.org. The **IHOPKC** community exists "to partner in the Great Commission by advancing 24/7 prayer with worship and proclaiming the beauty of Jesus and His glorious return." The twenty-four-hour-a-day prayer and worship has continued for the past twenty-five years.

Appendix E
Ten Ways to Become a More Missional Church

Many churches want to improve their mission engagement. These are some proven ways to do so:

1. Leadership

As with so many other things, so much rises and falls with leadership. Little can happen in the local church without the active support and participation of the senior pastor and governing board. If the pastor is mission-minded, the church will be also.

2. Prayer

Since the mission is God's mission, prayer is essential for local church mission engagement. Corporate prayer and individual prayers for the coming kingdom are the essential foundation for all the mission efforts.

3. On-Going Education

Teaching about the mission both from the pulpit and in Christian education classes is essential to maintain mission engagement.

4. A Sending and Support Structure

A missions team or missions committee ideally should include a leader from the church's governing body. This team will take the lead in recruiting and providing for the missionary family's financial, prayer, and moral support in coordination with the sending agency.

5. A Church Missions Manual

As the church's mission engagement develops, the team should compose a mission purpose statement in coordination with the church's leadership team.

6. A Policy Statement

The church should develop a policy statement to define the goals, policies, and procedures for partnering with the families and individuals in the field. The church may find it helpful to create and maintain a concise missions manual with a clear focus, such as emphasizing bringing the gospel to those who have not heard (Rom. 15:20).

7. Integration with Church Programs

In order to maintain a missional focus and engagement, missions should be integrated into the life of the local church. Missions can be integrated into children's ministries, Christian education, preaching, home groups, the prayer team, and communications media.

8. Mission Awareness Program

The missions team can be intentional about keeping the mission of the church in front of the congregation and report the latest news and prayer needs of the missionaries on the field.

9. Budget Priority

Since carrying out the Lord's mission is a high priority, we should reflect that in our annual budgets. Some churches find that supporting fewer missionaries but providing a higher level of support and a deeper partnership is more effective than a less focused approach.

10. Engage

There are many ways for local churches to engage in the mission God brings to our doorstep. Migrants and immigrants present a God-given opportunity to share the love of Christ with those who have not heard. English as a Second Language (ESL) is a time-honored way to serve our neighbors locally as well as on the field. Relationships develop through such service and these relationships can serve as the context for sharing the gospel. Other ways to engage include practicing hospitality, frequenting ethnic establishments, serving international students, and visiting world religion sites. Visiting a local mosque can be an effective way to open up relationships with Muslim friends. You will likely be warmly welcomed as you reach out with goodwill. Friends from the Middle East often love to talk about religion as much as Americans love to talk about sports, and this provides an opportunity to share the faith.

For more, see www.vineyardusa.org/how-to-be-missional-in-your-church/.

Appendix F
World Missions Resources

Books

Adriana Carranca, *Soul by Soul: The Evangelical Mission to Spread the Gospel to Muslims*. New York: Columbia Global Reports, 2024.

Brother Yun and Paul Hattaway, *Heavenly Man*. Grand Rapids: Kregel Publications, 2020.

Christopher J. H. Wright, *The Mission of God: Unlocking the Bible's Grand Narrative*. Downers Grove: InterVarsity Press, 2006.

Gina Zurlo, *Global Christianity: A Guide to the World's Largest Religion from Afghanistan to Zimbabwe*. Grand Rapids: Zondervan Academic, 2022.

Jason Mandryk and Molly Wall, editors. *Window on the World: An Operation World Prayer Resource. (Revised)*. Westmont: InterVarsity, 2018.

John Piper, *Let the Nations Be Glad!: The Supremacy of God in Missions*. Ada: Baker Academic, 2022. "Missions exist because worship doesn't."

Matthew Niermann, ed., *State of the Great Commission: Report prepared for Lausanne Global Congress*. Seoul-Incheon: Lausanne Movement, 2024 https://drive.google.com/file/d/1tLa-g2VBq44n4c6codxcCdzNkWzjUoAK/view.

Patrick Johnstone, *Serving God in a Migrant Crisis*. Downer's Grove: InterVarsity, 2018.

Sue Eenigenburg and Eva Burkholder, *Grit to Stay Grace to Go: Staying Well in Cross-Cultural Ministry*. Pasadena: William Carey Publishing, 2023.

Tim Keesee, *A Company of Heroes: Portraits from the Gospel's Global Advance.* Wheaton: Crossway, 2019.

Websites

Back to Jerusalem backtojerusalem.com

The Chinese house church movement has a vision to evangelize the unreached from the eastern provinces of China westward towards Jerusalem. Birthed among Chinese Christians in the 1920s, the Chinese house church movement has been battle-hardened by persecution and equipped by God to bring the gospel through the 10/40 Window from the Great Wall of China to the walls of Jerusalem.

William Carey Publishing www.missionbooks.org

Excellent source of books about missions. "With a sense of divine urgency and purpose, William Carey Publishing publishes resources that edify, equip, and empower disciples of Jesus to make disciples of Jesus and prompt breakthrough among unreached peoples."

IAM www.i-am.org

Useful articles and information about missions.

Joshua Project www.joshuaproject.net

The Joshua Project vision is "to see God glorified through an abundance of Christ followers within every people group. Its mission is to highlight peoples and places with the least access or response to the gospel so the Body of Christ can prioritize its prayer and mission efforts." Great source of information about the progress of the gospel in various countries and people groups.

Operation World www.operationworld.org

Country specific information, books, and prayer resources.

Lausanne Movement www.lausanne.org

"The Lausanne Movement has been at the forefront of global missions through fostering Christian collaboration, platforming missional strategy, and equipping leaders and influencers to fulfill the Great Commission."

Lausanne Action Hub https://collaborate.lausanne.org/

Join with like-minded teams and individuals to collaborate on important gaps and opportunities in seeing the Great Commission fulfilled.

Missionbooks www.missionbooks.org

An excellent source of missions books by Paul Hattaway and other top missions authors.

Mission Guide www.missionguide.global

Lists hundreds of short-term mission opportunities and offers a search by time, region, and activity. A useful way to find the right short-term mission for you.

Mission Frontiers www.missionfrontiers.org/

Mission to North American (Presbyterian Church in America) ESL training. This website lists in-person and online training opportunities to learn how to teach ESL (English as a Second Language). https://resources.pcamna.org/resource/esl-ministries_eslevents/

Stratus Index https://globe.stratus.earth/en/globe-explorer/

Stratus is a tool to equip the global church. It endeavors to prepare us to accomplish the Great Commission. Interactive globe interface.

Podcasts

Back to Jerusalem

Amazing and convicting accounts of how God is using the Chinese house church movement to bring the gospel to the unreached.

https://www.youtube.com/c/BackToJerusalem

backtojerusalem.com/podcast/

https://open.spotify.com/show/2hDW4UPsMWnok-P0C18nQNH

podcasts.apple.com/us/podcast/the-back-to-jerusalem-podcast/id1086176943

Apps

Jesus Film App (IOS, Android)

Shares the Jesus Film and related videos in 1,800 languages. Searchable by Bible story. This is an excellent evangelism tool because you can travel to the most remote areas of the world and cast the video onto a compatible smart TV from your smartphone.

5fish (IOS, Android)

Another very useful app for reaching the unreached. This app from Global Recordings has gospel messages in over 6,800 languages. First, download the app, then click on the languages of interest and download the message of interest. Take it on your next trip or use it with your international neighbor. You can share the gospel story with anyone from virtually any language group.

YouVersion Bible app (iOS, Android, Voice)

This has the entire Bible in 2,062 versions (1,372 languages). Useful for devotions, learning, and sharing.

Notes

1. Keller, *Prodigal Prophet*, 7.
2. Joshua Project, "Country: Iran."
3. Johnson, "Mission," in *World Christian Encyclopedia Online*.
4. The estimates of the numbers of unreached peoples in the world vary according to the definitions used and the methods of data collection and statistical analysis.
5. Joshua Project, "Global Dashboard."
6. Johnstone, *The Church is Bigger*, 80.
7. Barna, "51% of Churchgoers Don't Know of the Great Commission."
8. Niermann, *State of the Great Commission*.
9. Project42, "The Stats."
10. Lewis, "Clarifying the Remaining Frontier Mission Task."
11. Barrett, "World Christian Trends Table," 20-3.
12. The same WCTT survey reveals that $86 billion is lost to church-related fraud.
13. Gordon-Conwell, "Status of Global Christianity, 2024."
14. Gordon-Conwell, "Status of Global Christianity, 2024."

15. Johnson, "Finance," in: *World Christian Encyclopedia Online*.
16. Richard Halverson as quoted by Alcorn, *Money*, 3.
17. Auburn University, "A Glossary of Political Economy Terms."
18. Wikipedia, "Russian Orthodox Church."
19. Wikipedia, "Russian Orthodox Church."
20. Wikipedia, "Patriarch Kirill of Moscow."
21. CNN, "Dying for your country brings you to heaven, says Russian Patriarch."
22. Time, "Russia's War Against Evangelicals."
23. Patrick Johnstone, "Can Missions Thrive in an Age of Restrictions?" unpublished paper via email to the author, September 16, 2024.
24. Piper, *God-Entranced Vision*, 17.
25. Wikipedia, "William Tyndale."
26. Edwards, "Tyndale's Betrayal and Death."
27. Wikipedia, "Joint Declaration on the Doctrine of Justification."
28. Of course the *Joint Declaration* does not necessarily imply that every member of the Catholic Church has adopted a biblical and evangelical position on justification. However, it does mean that there are some in that branch of the Church, including some at the highest levels, who understand that salvation is a gift, and can serve as partners in inter-denominational mission partnerships.
29. Johnstone, *The Church is Bigger*, 33–80.
30. Johnstone, *The Church is Bigger*, 65.
31. Johnstone, *The Church is Bigger*, 48.
32. Douglas, *New Bible Dictionary*, 61.
33. Douglas, *New Bible Dictionary*, 61.

34. In answer to Q 191, "What do we pray for in the second petition?", the Catechism includes praying ". . . that the kingdom of sin and Satan may be destroyed, the gospel propagated throughout the world, the Jews called, the fullness of the Gentiles brought in . . ."

In 1903, the Presbyterian Church in the United States added Chapter 35, "Of the Gospel," which included the statement that "all believers are, therefore, under obligation to sustain the ordinance of the Christian religion where they are already established, and to contribute by their prayer, gifts, and personal efforts to the extension of the kingdom of Christ throughout the whole earth." However, some conservative Reformed denominations rejected the addition of this chapter on theological grounds. See "Westminster Confession of Faith Chapter 35," reformedchristianmuse.wordpress.com.

35. Legacyicons, "The Didache."
36. Johnstone, *The Church is Bigger*, 54.
37. ESV, "New Testament Timeline."
38. Johnstone, *The Church is Bigger*, 68.
39. Gonzales, *Christianity*, 98–99.
40. Johnstone, *The Church is Bigger*, 67.
41. Ma, "A Radical Vision of the Whole Church."
42. Davies, "The Great Commission from Calvin to Carey."
43. Carey, *Enquiry*, 9.
44. Baldwin, *Mears*, 225–255.
45. Migliazzo, *Mother of Modern Evangelicalism*, 151–152.
46. Hesselgrave, *Planting Churches*, 20.
47. I Corinthians 12:15–26.
48. Generationword, "Timeline of Acts."

49. Lovelace, *Dynamics*, 146.

50. Lovelace, *Dynamics*, 145.

51. Gibson, "Jonathan Edwards: A Missionary?"

52. Wikipedia, "Moravian Slaves."

53. Piper, "At the Price of God's Own Blood."

54. Joshua Project, "Global Summary."

55. Spoiledmilks, "The Farewell Discourse (John 13-17)."

56. Pressbook, "Jonathan Edwards."

57. Carson, *John*, 569.

58. Wikipedia, "Joint Declaration on the Doctrine of Justification."

59. A wider discussion about the Catholic Church's positions on justification is beyond the scope of this book. Certainly, the *Joint Declaration on Justification* asserted a position that is consistent with the Pauline position and that of the Reformed church and many Protestant branches. However, it would appear that work remains to be done to fully reconcile the *Declaration* with earlier documents, such as the *Catechism of the Catholic Church, Second Edition*.

60. Lausanne, "Lausanne Covenant."

61. Lausanne, "Manila Manifesto."

62. Black, "The Downward Path of Jesus."

63. Ross, "In Essentials Unity."

64. Wikipedia, "Toronto Blessing."

65. Psalm 133, "Peter Hocken—Meeting with the future Pope," 01–14:35.

66. Wooden, "Reformation at 500: Christians see they are brothers, sisters, pope says."

67. Piper, "You Shall Receive Power . . . For Mission."

68. Wisevoter, "Countries Currently at War."

69. Scougal, *The Life of God*, 3.

70. "He was foreknown before the foundation of the world but was made manifest in the last times for the sake of you . . ." (1 Peter 1:20), ". . . he chose us in him before the foundation of the world, that we should be holy and blameless before him" (Ephesians 1:4).

71. Keller, "Work," 01-36:21.

72. Goodreads, "Timothy J. Keller Quotes."

73. Koser, "Migration, Displacement and the Arab Spring."

74. Wikipedia, "Transformative Learning."

75. CBN News, "Ex-Terrorist Confirms Mass Visions of Jesus in Gaza," 01–6:40.

76. Wilson, *More to Be Desired than Gold*, 77.

77. 9marks, "Jonathan Edwards, Revival, and the Necessary Means of Prayer."

78. Gen. 31:7, Lev. 26:26, Ruth 4:2, etc.

79. Johnstone, *The Church is Bigger*, 80.

80. Edwards, *A Humble Attempt*, 64.

81. Edwards, *A Humble Attempt*, 7.

82. Zurlo, "World Christianity and Mission 2020: Ongoing Shift to the Global South," 80.

83. Lausanne, "The Lausanne Covenant."

84. Ma, "A Radical Vision."

85. Ma, "A Radical Vision."

86. Zurlo, "World Christianity."

87. Peterman, "My Disabled Body Proclaims the Gospel."

88. Lovelace, 151.

89. NBC, "John Sculley: What I learned from Steve Jobs."

BIBLIOGRAPHY

9marks. "Jonathan Edwards, Revival, and the Necessary Means of Prayer." Accessed December 18, 2023. https://www.9marks.org/article/jonathan-edwards-revival-and-the-necessary-means-of-prayer/.

Alcorn, Randy. *Money, Possessions and Eternity.* Tyndale, 1989.

Baldwin, Ethel May. *Henrietta Mears*. Regal, 1966.

Barrett, David B. and Johnson, Todd M. "World Christian Trends Table." William Carey Library, 2001. https://static1.squarespace.com/static/4f661fde24ac1097e013deea/t/61fad19d0bbaad2bcc465978/1643827613106/WCT_Table20-3.pdf.

Barna. "51% of Churchgoers Don't Know of the Great Commission." Accessed March 28, 2023. https://www.barna.com/research/half-churchgoers-not-heard-great-commission/.

Black, David. "The Downward Path of Jesus: Moving Beyond the Sunday-Centric Church." (July 20, 2015). https://www.daveblackonline.com/downward_path_of_jesus.htm.

Carson, D. A. ed., *The Gospel According to John*. Eerdmans, 1991.

Carey, William. *An Enquiry Into the Obligations of Christians to Use Means for the Conversion of the Heathens.* Leicester, 1792. https://www.decadeofpentecost.org/wp-content/uploads/2015/08/An-Enquiry-into-the-Obligation-of-Christians-to-Use-Means-for-the-Conversion-of-the-Heathens.pdf.

CBN. "Ex-Terrorist Confirms Mass Visions of Jesus in Gaza." Accessed January 22, 2024. https://www.youtube.com/watch?v=eh1wQIJC5jY.

Clifford, Catherine. "Former Apple CEO John Sculley: What I learned from Steve Jobs." *CNBC*. Accessed May 28, 2025. https://www.cnbc.com/2018/05/29/what-ex-apple-pepsi-ceo-john-sculley-learned-from-steve-jobs.html.

CNE. "Dying for your country brings you to heaven, says Russian Patriarch." Accessed June 17, 2024. https://cne.news/article/1756-dying-for-your-country-brings-you-to-heaven-says-russian-patriarch.

Davies, R.E. "The Great Commission from Calvin to Carey." *Gospel Studies*. Accessed May 28, 2025. https://www.gospelstudies.org.uk/biblicalstudies/pdf/evangel/14-2_044.pdf.

Douglas, J. D., ed. *New Bible Dictionary*. InterVarsity, 1982.

Edwards, Brian H. "Tyndale's Betrayal and Death." *Christian History*, no. 16 (1987). https://christianhistoryinstitute.org/magazine/article/tyndales-betrayal-and-death.

Edwards, Jonathan. *A Humble Attempt to Promote the Agreement and Union of God's People Throughout the World in Extraordinary Prayer For a Revival Of Religion And The Advancement Of God's Kingdom On Earth, According To Scriptural Promises And Prophecies Of The*

Last Time. Boston, 1747. http://name.umdl.umich.edu/N04757.0001.001.

ESV. "New Testament Timeline." Accessed September 14, 2023. https://www.esv.org/resources/esv-global-study-bible/chart-40-00-nt-timeline/.

Generationword. "Timeline of Acts." Accessed April 24, 2024. https://www.generationword.com/bible_school_notes/Timeline%20of%20Acts.htm.

Gibson, Jonathan. "Jonathan Edwards: A Missionary?" Accessed November 26, 2023. https://www.thegospelcoalition.org/themelios/article/jonathan-edwards-a-missionary/.

Gonzales, Justo L. *The Story of Christianity, Volume I*. Harper & Row, 1984.

Goodreads. "Timothy J. Keller Quotes." Accessed May 28, 2025. https://www.goodreads.com/author/quotes/847789.Timothy_J_Keller.

Gordon-Conwell. "Status of Global Christianity, 2024, in the Context of 1900–2050." Accessed May 28, 2025. https://static1.squarespace.com/static/4f661fde24ac1097e013deea/t/65bd27b23fbd8e4b9cf7e1d0/1706895282534/Status-of-Global-Christianity-2024.pdf.

Hesselgrave, David. *Planting Churches Cross-Culturally*. Baker, 1980.

Hocken, Peter. "Meeting with the future Pope." Accessed December 4, 2023. https://www.youtube.com/watch?v=xRpoH004o80.

Johnson, Paul M. *A Glossary of Political Economy Terms*. Auburn University, 2016. https://webhome.auburn.edu/~johnspm/gloss/.

Johnson, Todd M., and Zurlo, Gina A., eds., "Finance" in *World Christian Encyclopedia Online*. Accessed on February 12, 2024. http://dx.doi.org/10.1163/2666-6855_WCEO_COM_0107.

Johnson, Todd M., and Zurlo, Gina A., eds., "Mission" in *World Christian Encyclopedia Online*. Accessed on February 12, 2024, http://dx.doi.org/10.1163/2666-6855_WCEO_COM_0107.

Joshua Project. "Country: Iran." Accessed March 28, 2023. https://www.joshuaproject.net/countries/ir.

Joshua Project. "Global Dashboard." Accessed March 28, 2023. https://www.joshuaproject.net.

Johnstone, Patrick. *The Church is Bigger Than You Think: The Unfinished Work of World Evangelisation.* Christian Focus Publications, 1998.

Keller, Timothy. *The Prodigal Prophet.* Viking, 2018.

Keller, Timothy. "Work." Sermon Video. May 31, 2023. https://www.youtube.com/watch?v=tpTQUpl_9bA.

Koser, Khalid. "Migration, Displacement and the Arab Spring." Accessed April 2, 2023. https://www.brookings.edu/articles/migration-displacement-and-the-arab-spring-lessons-to-learn/.

Lausanne. "The Lausanne Covenant." July, 1975. https://lausanne.org/statement/lausanne-covenant.

Lausanne. "The Manilla Manifesto." July 20, 1989. https://lausanne.org/statement/the-manila-manifesto.

Legacyicons. *The Didache.* Accessed October 21, 2024. https://legacyicons.com/content/didache.pdf.

Lewis, R.W., "Clarifying the Remaining Frontier Mission Task." *International Journal of Frontier Missions* 35, no. 4 (2018) 1–15. https://static1.squarespace.com/

static/4f661fde24ac1097e013deea/t/5bcfe6b18165f5cc5f820e58/1540351671087/IJFM_35_4-Lewis.pdf.

Lovelace, Richard F. *Dynamics of Spiritual Life: An Evangelical Theology of Renewal*. Inter-Varsity, 1979.

Ma, Wonsuk. "A Radical Vision of the Whole Church," Lausanne Global Analysis 12, no. 3 (2023). https://lausanne.org/content/lga/2023-05/a-radical-vision-of-the-whole-church.

Migliazzo, Arlin C. *Mother of Modern Evangelicalism*. Eerdmans, 2020.

Niermann, Matthew, ed., *State of the Great Commission*. Lausanne Movement, 2024. https://drive.google.com/file/d/1tLa-g2VBq44n4c6codxcCdzNkWzjUoAK/view.

Peterman, Amar D. "My Disabled Body Proclaims the Gospel." *Sojourners* (March, 2022). https://sojo.net/articles/my-disabled-body-proclaims-gospel.

Piper, John. "At the Price of God's Own Blood." Accessed May 28, 2025. https://www.desiringgod.org/messages/at-the-price-of-gods-own-blood.

Piper, John. "You Shall Receive Power…For Mission." Accessed December 5, 2023. https://www.desiringgod.org/messages/you-shall-receive-power-for-mission.

Piper, John and Taylor, Justin, eds. *A God-Entranced Vision of All Things*. Crossway, 2004.

Pressbook. "Jonathan Edwards." Accessed June 5, 2024. https://cwi.pressbooks.pub/americanliterature/chapter/jonathan-edwards/.

Project42partners. "The Stats." Accessed March 28, 2024, https://www.project42partners.org/stats.

Robinson, Spenser. "Jesus' Farewell Discourse in John 13–17." Accessed November 27, 2023. https://spoiledmilks.com/2024/03/28/jesus-farewell-discourse-john-13-17/.

Ross, Mark. "In Essentials Unity, In Non-Essentials Liberty, In All Things Charity." *Ligonier*, September 1, 2009. Accessed December 4, 2023. https://www.ligonier.org/learn/articles/essentials-unity-non-essentials-liberty-all-things.

Scougal. Henry. *The Life of God in the Soul of Man*. London, 1677. Accessed December 5, 2023, https://ccel.org/ccel/scougal/life/life.ii.html.

Time. "Russia's War Against Evangelicals." Accessed June 17, 2024. https://time.com/6969273/russias-war-against-evangelicals/.

Wikipedia. "Joint Declaration on the Doctrine of Justification." Accessed November 30, 2023. https://en.wikipedia.org/wiki/Joint_Declaration_on_the_Doctrine_of_Justification.

Wikipedia. "Moravian Slaves." Accessed November 29, 2023. https://en.wikipedia.org/wiki/Moravian_slaves.

Wikipedia. "Russian Orthodox Church." Accessed June 17, 2024. https://en.wikipedia.org/wiki/Russian_Orthodox_Church.

Wikipedia. "Patriarch Kirill of Moscow." Accessed June 17, 2024. https://en.wikipedia.org/wiki/Patriarch_Kirill_of_Moscow.

Wikipedia. "Toronto Blessing." Accessed May 28, 2025. https://en.wikipedia.org/wiki/Toronto_Blessing.

Wikipedia. "Transformative Learning." Accessed September 30, 2024. https://en.wikipedia.org/wiki/Transformative_learning.

Wikipedia. "William Tyndale." Accessed May 28, 2025. https://en.wikipedia.org/wiki/William_Tyndale.

Wilson, J. Christy Jr. *More to Be Desired Than Gold: True Stories Told by Christy Wilson.* Gordon-Conwell, 1998.

Wisevoter. "Countries Currently at War." Accessed December 5, 2023. https://wisevoter.com/country-rankings/countries-currently-at-war/.

Wooden, Cindy. "Reformation at 500: Christians say they are brothers, sisters, pope says." *Cruxnow.* Accessed December 4, 2023. https://cruxnow.com/vatican/2017/10/reformation-500-christians-see-brothers-sisters-pope-says.

World Population Review. "Countries Currently at War." Accessed May 28, 2025. https://worldpopulationreview.com/country-rankings/countries-currently-at-war.

Zurlo, Gina et al. "World Christianity and Mission 2020: Ongoing Shift to the Global South." *International Bulletin of Mission Research* 44, no. 1 (2019). https://journals.sagepub.com/doi/10.1177/2396939319880074.

About the Author

J. CHRISTOPHER EVANS is a creative who uses the arts to glorify his Savior and advance the gospel. He is a writer, painter, and founder of a media ministry for the unreached. He uses visual arts to highlight unreached peoples. Serving as a "tentmaker," a self-supporting witness, he uses writing to encourage recovering the truth that mission engagement is part of following Christ. He had the privilege of serving as the chairman of the strategy committee of a denominational mission board. A Presbyterian elder, he attended Gordon-Conwell Theological Seminary where he was awarded the Olive Branch Prize for dedication to world missions. He did additional work at Harvard University.

www.ingramcontent.com/pod-product-compliance
Lightning Source LLC
Chambersburg PA
CBHW070848050426
42453CB00012B/2087